The Way Home
On the Poetry of Colette Inez

The Way Home
On the Poetry of Colette Inez

Edited by Kevin Bezner

Word Press

Copyright © 2003 by Kevin Bezner

Published by Word Press
P.O. Box 541106
Cincinnati, OH 45254-1106

Poetry Editor: Kevin Walzer
Business Editor: Lori Jareo

Visit us on the web at www.word-press.com

ISBN: 0-9717371-3-4
LCCN: 2002114681

Typeset in Lapidary by WordTech Communications, Cincinnati, OH

Contents

Preface / 7

Chronology / 9

A Poem
Colette Inez *My Mother and Cartography* / 13

A Memoir
Colette Inez *Visitors* / 17

Interviews
"Open to Adventures" / 25
Jim Gorman "The Power of Words" / 31
Kevin Walzer "Rallying Cry" / 43
Kevin Bezner *The Way Home: A Conversation with Colette Inez* / 47

Essays
Sharon Klander *Worlds Made with Words: The Poetry of Colette Inez* / 55
John Harvey *An Unfocused Star* / 61
Kathleen Reilly *The Mirror and the Map: Colette Inez and the Orphan's Poetic Search* / 67
E. Barnsley Brown *"And I will have my say": Mother Loss and Mother Tongues in Colette Inez's* CLEMENCY / 75
Susan Sindall CLEMENCY: *Poems by Colette Inez* / 81
Lili Corbus Bezner *The Image as Memory: The Use of Photography and Painting in Colette Inez's Poetry* / 85

Reviews
Rosellen Brown *Review of* ALIVE AND TAKING NAMES / 95
Robert McDowell *Review of* ALIVE AND TAKING NAMES / 99
David Lawson *A Shifting Center of Poetic Gravity* / 101
Robert DeMott *Recent Poetry* / 105
Robert Schultz *"Full Throated Assurance"* / 109
Scott Edward Anderson *"The Agony and Enlightenment of a Complete Life"* / 111
Steven Styers *"The Reconstruction of a Life"* / 115

For Further Reading / 119

Preface

The words of David Del Tredici, composer of *Miz Inez Sez*, a song cycle written to five poems by Colette Inez, offer clear statements about why Inez's poetry is so important to us. Tredici is quoted in the May 11, 2001 issue of the *Bay Area Reporter* as saying, "As had James Joyce, so now does Colette Inez touch my damaged Catholic nerve, which is a spot full of hurt and, paradoxically, humor—that effective, if temporary, antidote to pain."

The hurt that Inez suffered as a cradle Catholic, albeit an illegitimate one, was what initially made her a poet and gave her a story to tell. It is the story that initially drew many of us to her poetry, because we could explore her hurt and our own, whether Catholic or not, at the same time.

As the daughter of a priest and a scholar, Inez was rejected by a father ordained a Monsignor the year of her birth and a mother Inez suggests was too isolated a person to have raised a child, a woman in awe of her lover but not in love with him. Within ten days of her birth, Inez was placed in a Catholic orphanage, where she suffered deprivation. She learned harsher lessons when sent to live with alcoholic and abusive foster parents in the United States at the age of eight.

What is most remarkable about Inez is that she has explored this story and her hurt and yet has never became bitter or rancorous. Instead, after such a difficult start, she has created a joyful life through poetry and in her own stable marriage to Saul A. Stadtmauer.

In her poetry, Inez's personal story carries on what R.W.B. Lewis called, in *The American Adam*, the "lively and creative dialogue" entered into by American writers of the nineteenth century. These writers, he says, attempted to define what it meant to live in a new world and a new country. "The American myth saw life and history as just beginning," he writes. "It described the world as starting up again under fresh initiative, in a divinely granted second chance for the human race, after the first start had been so disastrously fumbled in the darkening Old World."

Inez's story starts in Europe, but it continues in America. While she created a response to the world her parents gave her—and in doing so transformed them and herself into literary characters in the story she was compelled to tell—she eventually won clemency from that story, as she calls it, and transformed herself in the process.

In the act of transforming herself, Inez turned to art, nature here on earth and in the sky, cultures far different from her own, and the love of her husband—all of which, in addition to the story of her parents, make up the themes of her poetry.

In ending her book *Clemency* with the poem "Transformations," she informs us that creating a self in poetry has led her to a new state of self creation—"We will hide in a damp cocoon and start again"—after many years of exploration.

She is done, she is telling us, with the story of her innocence, the years she spent obsessed with the mystery of her conception, the years she spent defined as the progeny of a fallen man and woman. If hers is not a home of forgiveness, it is one of understanding and reconciliation. Above all else, it is a home of love.

We may have been drawn to her poetry initially because of her story, the life she had to endure and overcome. But we return to this story, and await the new story that is unfolding now, because of her indomitable spirit, her endurance and acceptance, her love of life and language, and her remarkable joy.

Kevin Bezner
Charlotte, North Carolina
June, 2002 and March, 2003

Chronology

1931	Born June 23 in Brussels, Belgium
1938	Placed in a foster home in the United States
1939	Sent to the United States to live with foster parents
1961	B.A., Hunter College of the City University of New York
1961–1971	Teacher, New York City
1962	Instructor, American Language Institute, New York University
	National League of American PEN Women poetry award
1964	Marries Saul A. Stadtmauer, a freelance writer, on July 26
1969	Osgood Warren national first prize award, Poetry Society of New England
1972	*The Woman Who Loved Worms*
	Marion Reedy National Award, Poetry Society of America
	Great Lakes Colleges Association first prize book award for *The Woman Who Loved Worms*.
1973–1983	Member of faculty, The New School
1974	National Endowment for the Arts Fellowship
	Reedy Memorial Award, Poetry Society of America
1975	New York State Creative Artists Public Service (CAPS) fellowship
	Visiting Professor, Kalamazoo College—she will be asked back six more times through 1993
	Beck Lecturer, Denison University
1976	Kreymborg National Poetry Award, Poetry Society of America
1977	*Alive and Taking Names*
1978	Visiting Professor, Hunter College
1979	Elected to Governing Board of the Poetry Society of America
1980	Rockefeller Foundation Fellowship, Residency in Bellagio, Italy
	Yaddo Foundation Fellowship—she will receive four more fellowships through 1990
1982	Ragdale Foundation residency; keynoted 1984 conference
1983	*Eight Minutes from the Sun*
	Begins teaching in the Columbia University Undergraduate Writing Program
	Virginia Center for the Creative Arts Fellowship—she will receive five more fellowships through 1994

	Faculty, Southampton Writers' Conference; repeated twice through 1991
1985	Guggenheim Foundation Fellowship
1986	Pushcart Prize for "What Are the Days?"
	Faculty, Wesleyan Writers Conference
	Faculty, Southern Methodist University Writers' Conference
1987	Elected to Hunter College Hall of Fame
1988	*Family Life*
	National Endowment for the Arts Fellowship
1990	Visiting Professor, Ohio University
1991	Millay Colony for the Arts, Norma Millay Fellow honoree
1992	Poet in Residence, Bucknell University
	Faculty, Aspen Writers Conference
1993	*Getting Under Way*
	Poet in Residence, Colorado State University, Fort Collins
1994	*Naming the Moons*
	For Reasons of Music
	MacDowell Colony Fellowship
	Faculty, Naropa Institute Writers Conference
1995	Faculty, Antionch Writers Workshop
1998	*Clemency*
	Visiting Professor, Cornell University
	Pushcart Prize for "Monologue of the Falconer's Wife"
2000	"Miz Inez Sez" by David Del Tredici, a song cycle written to five of her poems, is performed at The Miller Theater at Columbia University
	Visiting Professor, Colgate University
2001	*Greatest Hits: 1970–2000*
	Faculty, Centrum's 28th Annual Port Townsend Writers' Conference
	"Miz Inez Sez" is released on the CRI compact disk, *Secret Music*. Alex Ross writes in *The New Yorker* that it "may be the best new-music album of the year."
2002	Medway Institute residency
	Completes *The Letter Before A*
	Arons Poet, Newcombe College, Tulane University residency
2003	*The Secret of M. Dulong,* prose memoir, accepted for publication by University of Wisconsin Press

A Poem

Colette Inez

My Mother and Cartography

I scan your face as if it were the map of France,
a five-pointed star. Do I resemble you
in the foothills of the Pyrenees, in Tarbes, Lourdes, Pau?
Does your northern point in Dunquerque hug the Belgian
border where you hauled me into birth? A forehead's
width, do we share that? Not your hairline in Brittany
and Alsace, cheekbones in Poitou and Chalon, sly mouth
pursed in Aubusson. If I were to give my face to you
as a replica of France, would I have to explain:
here is my highest, lowest point, seasonal lakes, salt
flats, cascades, would you then be moved to look at me,
to speak my name here in your mother country?

I study your body as if it were the map of France,
and I, a cartographer learning your conversion scales,
permanent streams, principal rivers and roads. Where
do I favor you most? It's idle to deny your collarbone
in Picardie and the likeness of our throats.
Is it possible in Creuse or Allier I inhabited
your womb for the customary term, that our internal
boundaries were the same? Did you wonder, a daughter or
a son when I howled into the June air of Brabant,
north of a lowland country?

But you are not France nor am I your cartographer.
I never read your legs in Gascony and Dauphin, and
when we met north of Touquet, that first time, I didn't
measure your crosshatched lines, brackets poised
along your mouth, the distance you held in miles.
When you walked away, your feet didn't wade in Vence and Hendaye,
never idly rocked at low tide along the docks
of Menton or St. Jean de Luz in the southwestern cusp
of France's star. Your body, and face slowly made their way

from morning to morning in a cold country,
neither yours nor mine.

Years later, you won't read what I have to write,
my system of location drawn on paper and in ink. You sit
and look at the gravel pit where vineyards once grew
to the river's edge. You, gone back to your place of birth,
to Nerac, a physical world defined, east of Gironde,
west of Cestas, you, my mountain, my capital, my star,
my scholar mother now curling words in your mother tongue.
Shall I offer you the map of my forbearance, its hachures
and grids, time zones and rifts to be your keepsake in
the thinning years? I will address this gift to you
in your river house, my high-minded lady of France, you
who left me with the Belgian Sisters and now
present me to your tenants as a friend
from America, a far and marvelous country.

A Memoir

Colette Inez

Visitors

In a room that doubles as a study hall, I am isolated with a handful of other girls assigned to embroider and hem ladies' handkerchiefs whose final disposition is never quite clear although it has something to do with Africa. An older girl sitting next to me explains that money is raised for the missions on that continent through the sale of our guest towels, doilies, pillow cases and handkerchiefs.

On our classroom's pull-down map, Africa is an immense maze of blue, green, yellow, pink, and orange countries where I imagine palm trees sway in days of perpetual heat. But on this spring afternoon in Belgium, nuns seem almost immune to heat and the few times I notice a hanky lifted to mop a brow or tamp a nose, the cloth is a simple, unadorned square.

So it must be, I suppose, we labor for Africa. Our religious order, largely territorial, is in this case chosen to light the Dark Continent with the divine radiance of Christ whose carved figure on wall plaques emits gilded beams that seem to blaze beyond their frames.

Handkerchiefs, I think, may be sent off in the bulging pockets of our missionary Brothers to wave at the natives, to inspire and awe black converts with the delicacy of our handiwork in His name.

We mechanically ply our needles along the edges of the cloth, or cross stitch palm trees, fleurs-de-lis, swans, and windmills, distracted now and then by the buzz of adult voices in the corridor, the hum of talk from parents or relatives on weekly calls with their resident children.

On visitors day, we, the stitchers, are huddled away from the traffic with no explanation for our removal although we know well enough no one has come to share Sunday with us. Aren't we as worthy as Jeanne and Claude bounding ahead of Grandma and Grandpa, Uncle Paul, or Cousin so and so, in the yard outside the window, skimming a forbidden gift hoop between them? Don't we matter as much as Anne and her big boned blond relatives?

Patience, I tell myself, perhaps my own parents are missionaries detained in Tanganyika, Kenya, The Congo, ragged splashes of color in the rainbow of African nations I imagine separated by borders of brick walls or fences of iron spikes like those circling the institute where daily we discover the rules of worldly exclusion.

My parents, I muse, are gathering up gifts, an enormous horde of marvelous toys they're satisfied to bring me only when enough are collected to fill the cavernous refectory in which we children take our meals three times daily. The assembling of presents must take years to complete, but in the end how astonished Jeanne and Claude will be with my truckload of spinning tops and balls, dolls and jacks, blocks and pinwheels, train sets and cars, enough to share with everyone, should the nuns ever allow it.

Since no one speaks of them, my parents become the couple I must invent; their elegance or holiness is cut from snips and ends of fairy tales and religious parables. I embellish them with gossip the other wards magnify into elaborate chronicles, lies and facts garnished with fantasies of the King of Belgium and his beautiful queen. Mother and father are not missionaries but people of means who sleep in private berths on great ships and greet the day with pale clothes and large hats. Illustrated magazines show them stepping from glistening cars. Surely, they live joyously feasting on bon bons and sipping hot chocolate served to them from gold mugs. They are noble and speak politely to one another in hushed tones. When summoning servants, they say please and thank you very much. They never snap their fingers for attention or blow their noses loudly. Of this I am sure.

But this time, the hour of musing is interrupted by an unexpected event. A nun enters the room, brushes aside my thin pile of untrimmed linen, and leads me through a quiet corridor to a high ceilinged room furnished with several benches and hard backed chairs.

In a nondescript brown suit like that I'd sometimes seen worn by young lay teachers who came to instruct us in knitting and crocheting, a plain woman wearing a close fitting hat is seated, silently counting prayers on a rosary.

"She's your auntie from France," an old nun explains. An auntie? I am baffled by the introduction and brimming with questions about my parents. Who and where are they? When will they leave their pink or orange country and take me home? Why did they leave me here as a baby? Why?

She ignores my asking, and murmurs something about the weather, how unexpectedly warm it is. A deep line cuts the space between her eyes, large and gold flecked in the light. The nun wags an admonishing finger, ordering me to hold my tongue, to behave or know the reasons why. I am startled by her fierce scowl; it is a look to be taken seriously.

Impudence is corrected with a switch or a cane, and I have no trouble recalling the stinging pain of my last punishment for stealing a forbidden toy rattle from the infant ward. Sometimes I take secret pleasure in the rush of heat that floods my lower parts, the hidden ones we are not supposed to see or think about. We wear white panties under our muslin night gowns, and when we bathe we shiver on line, draped in rough towels that loosely cover us from waist to knees.

How somber and sad is this auntie. Oak brown smooth hair knotted in a tight bun, and clear olive skin so unlike my dark curls and pink complexion. Only her forehead is broad like mine. She is perfectly still and unsmiling. I cannot believe she ever fidgeted or squirmed when discovered in a lie or left damp crescents of sweat beneath the sleeves of her dress. That she might gnaw at her fingernails or stick out her tongue when a nun turned her back is unthinkable.

Holding a book of common prayer, she calmly asks me to kneel and pray with her. I obey but mumble an invocation by rote, distracted by her scent of strong soap of freshly laundered clothes. A pleasant odor, but I find little else to favor in this melancholy woman, her drab wool garments, her single gold tooth flashing like the gold crucifix she wears at her throat. Our visit ends as it began with a few ordinary words exchanged; obey the Sisters, pray to God for his compassion. Her departure seems as mysterious to me as her sudden arrival.

Some weeks later I meet her again in a dream in which her face floats towards me, lips parted, her gold tooth pulsing like a star reflected in water, and I try to touch the face, to stroke it but each time I approach and come close, it draws away from me. When I call out to Sister Paul, a stout, gap toothed nun known among us children for her heartiness, she stamps and waves her arms, cups her hands but cannot catch the drifting face, cannot hold it down for me or find the body that belongs to it. My French aunt. In the dream I again want to question her about my parents.

She returns the following year, and perhaps during a few succeeding years, again asking me to implore God to forgive our sins, to have patience and faith, to trust in the Lord when I incautiously speak of family. We kneel and pray. To press her for more information would be impertinent. As commanded by the nuns, guardians of propriety, I must wait to be spoken to.

My aunt, who is told by Sister Bernard we are studying the lives of the saints, examines what I learned. Saint Bathilde? Captured by Corsairs and sold as a slave. Saint Eulalie? Endured tortures and was burned alive on a pyre. Saint Georgette? Fasted every day and ceaselessly sent prayers to God. In a ratifying message from heaven, doves hovered over her remains during the burial. Eager to show off what I know, I am equally enthralled and oppressed by these stories of piety and sacrifice.

On one occasion she wears a maroon knit dress, and I stare raptly at her skin through the tiny windows between the stitches. The ordinariness of her flat brown laced-up shoes displeases me. I secretly crave a more fashionable relative the other children will admire me for having.

Once she brings a plaything, a stuffed bear or dog, and the nuns remind her of the Institute's inflexible rule, the prohibition against private ownership. Even our clothes are issued by the commissary and are not our own. Nor are rosaries and combs, underpants and shoes, night dresses and chamber pots. We are taught it is vain and agitating to prize personal possessions. Nuns say the children will squabble, fight over them.

As usual, the woman says little to me. I wonder if she feels disappointed as I am with our visits. In some important way, I believe I fail her, but I prefer not knowing how or precisely why.

Is my perversity at not pleasing her another flaw in my character, among faults which the nuns seem to take delight in proclaiming? Such as my stubborn refusal to clean the slimy mutton fat from my plate. And how I slothfully sit head in hands and drift into day dreams during lessons.

Or carnal acts. Sometimes after touching myself, sensing the tingle of my secret parts, the hand passes the long night between my thighs. Other disgusting habits. I pick my nose, swallow my fingernail parings, wipe away phlegm with the back of my hand. More unforgivably, I ignore God's presence in chapel. Narcissism and conceit. I brood on not being pretty, a woeful condition made clear by an attending nun I once overheard saying so to the auntie. "But she's quick to learn and clever with her hands."

I come to distrust what it is the Sisters think they know about me. I despise embroidering. Chantal sews a finer hem, and lovely blue eyed, blonde Marie cross stitches in neater rows. I am jealous of blonde girls and covet Anne's thick silky braids, envy her Sunday visitors, their noisy talk about hard times for Belgian farmers and rumors of another war.

I am told my auntie is not one of them, not of the farm. Her smooth hands and firm short nails resemble those of the studious nuns who later speak to me of her career as a scholar in French history. Medieval history. Yes, I understand this, know of Charlemagne, the song of Roland, Jeanne D'Arc and the French kings. We are taught French as well as Belgian history, I tell her.

During those few meetings, a question or two about my studies is followed by my quick answers. We have exhausted what I know about the lives of the saints, and she no longer wishes to hear me recite. Out of the corner of my eye I begin to perceive a stranger who might know nothing about my parents, and that must explain her elusiveness. She may be a distant relative so far removed from our family, its members are foreign to her.

"We are not put here on earth for pleasant times," this aunt likes to say to me. I sit demurely with crossed ankles, hands folded in my lap, and sneak glimpses of her long, mournful face.

Summer's fresh scent of mown grass drifts with fallen leaves into winter smells of cabbage soup, wet wool sleeves and socks filled with Christmas oranges. January,

February, gray sleet and rain. March, mud and crocuses.

An old diamond back turtle inching a path to a remembered meadow is discovered on its back. Sister Jerome, who mends the wings of birds, flips the creature over, sending it with a tap on its carapace along its lumbering journey. At recess, Jeanne, Marie, Anne and I intercept it and marvel at its plodding pace. Like that of Marie's grandmere who, too, has a crinkled neck and beak-like slit lips.

During occasional visits Marie's grandmother brings us magazines with pictures of women adorned in silk dresses, hair neatly waved under hats floating like halos of spring flowers. Loose jackets with butterflies on them. Women resplendent in long strands of pearls strolling in gardens on their country estates.

The images of that privileged world cling to me like a whiff of Lily of the Valley, a cologne worn by a well dressed woman who often visited little Jeanne-Pierre. I tailor them in my mind's eye to the motifs of the Institute, pin elegant replicas of high fashion on the statue of the Virgin Mother, so distant and prim in her nook on the chapel wall.

On a Sunday soon after Easter, while we attend a brief noontime service, my reverie of Mary in a cloche hat and flared print skirt is shattered by a tug on my uniform sleeve.

A younger girl, a message bearer, whispers astonishing news in my ear. "Two men have come for you." I am guided to the Mother Superior's office.

They stand casually near the door when I enter, not priests in long black gowns as I half expect, but two young civilians dressed stylishly in blue suits and white shirts. Only at a first communion or confirmation had I seen men dressed like this and even then it was not common.

One of the men, as handsome as a movie star, carries a black leather case. The other has an auburn mustache and bright blue eyes. Mother Superior introduces: "Colette, I wish you to meet Mr. Branigan and Mr. Bale from America."

America? I have seen that huge country on the map, learned to name some of its forty-eight states. I catch my breath, my heart pounds. Father! The thought rises as my eyes leap to the taller of the two, Mr. Bale, whose name is oddly different from my own, but whose calm and even features please me. I ignore his older, plainer friend, and with forced composure, ask the question.

Will he take me to my parents? No. Are they in Africa? Africa and America sound alike to me. No.

The strangers say they came only as companions for a long ship voyage, and tomorrow I will leave with them for America, pass through the iron gates behind which each day we children file like goslings from dormitory to wash room, from matinals in chapel, and on to the refectory. Then quick morning steps to the chapel followed by lunch and afternoon studies.

After supper, we regroup, all of us in our brown weekday uniforms marching to Vespers at dusk. Lights out at eight in the evening. Patterns of a measured life. In excitement and confusion over the prospect, I ask nothing more of the men about my family. If their mission is a secret covenant with others, even with the auntie to take me home at last, I have not been told.

Interviews

"Open to Adventures"

Crazy Horse, Number 14, November 1973

CRAZY HORSE: We like to begin our interviews by having the poet provide an autobiographical sketch of himself or herself. Would you do that?

COLETTE INEZ: The hard facts. I'm illegitimate according to law and improbable according to Catholic canons ... conceived in Paris to a medievalist mother and Jesuit father who discreetly hustled me to Brussels, Belgium, where I was born and reared in a Catholic home for children. Status: quasi-orphan. At age eight I was exported to the United States, a "package deal" covertly pre-arranged by my father who had died by this time. The package was misaddressed, and I landed in a foster home instead. Years in Long Island, New York, time in Cleveland, Ohio. After high school I was a telephone operator, file clerk, factotum, secretary, office temporary—survival jobs while drifting through the Beat scene of Greenwich Village. Then hiking through Europe with a rucksack looking for and finding my mother. No welcome mat there. Accumulations, accretions and finally enough confidence to earn a nightschool degree at Hunter College in 1961. New adventures teaching illiterates to read and write, teaching English as a second language in the New York City anti-poverty program. Married and remarried, I've settled into the present and try to stay amazed.

CH: Would you care to talk about the relationship, if you feel there is any, between your European background and your poetry? Do you feel you have a certain distance from the American experience (yet a closeness to it) that is helpful? (I sense a certain internationalism in your book.)

CI: Events have definitely tipped the scales towards this side of the Atlantic. I've eaten my share of American pie. Transplanted Midwesterners from Iowa and Illinois, my foster parents were grandchildren of Scot coalminers and German farmers. My foster grandmother's aunt and uncle were killed by a Cheyenne war party. I lived in Cleveland in the forties with people who were nearly eighty. Uncle Ed, itinerant piano tuner, Aunt Kate who dusted at midnight, and addled Aunt Agnes who left her room only for meals. Cleveland of that day was the port of great migrations from the South. As the war ended, we were the sole whites on the block. But around the corner was Prague and Cracow, and I read letters for illiterate Czech and Polish ladies for a nickel. America, America, and not much melting anywhere. One of my steadfast loves was geography—meridians, latitudes, peninsulas and place names in particular: Katmandu, Djibouti, Kuala Lumpur. Also atlases and globes. European history and literature perhaps because I unconsciously hoped that by knowing these things, I might through the haze of events locate my life and origins.

CH: When I first read your book, I sensed the presence of Emily Dickinson there. She seemed a kind of friendly ghost hovering over many of the poems. Then I read the interview with you in *Yes, A Magazine of Poetry* and discovered that she was indeed your first and strongest influence. Could you tell us what you feel you learned from her and why she commanded your attention as she did? Do you still read her?

CI: From Emily I learned that large minds can live in small places. Perched in her rooms at Amherst, she moved through entire topographies of pain, celebration, insight. Listen to this: "The heart asks pleasure first/And then excuse from pain/And then, those little anodynes that deaden suffering." A compressed biography of the human race. It was love at first sight when I read her "vats upon the Rhine," "Belshazar's correspondent/concluded and begun," "auto-da-fe and judgement are nothing to the bee," and romantic names: Van Dieman's land, Circassian, all those orchids in her garden of bees and clover rows. What else? I learned that one could rhyme "green" with "entertain," "sun" with "platoon," "keel" with "beautiful," a brimming lexicon of assonance and consonance. I also learned to hear music on a slant as opposed to the vertical notes of "yellow-jello" rhymes. I'm still learning the value of "zero at the bone," getting maximal rings from a minimal stone flung into water. I reread Emily last week after a lapse of ten years, and although her quaintness occasionally irks, the "wizard fingers" still strike full octaves in my mind.

CH: Would you choose a poem from your book that you're particularly fond of and comment on it?

CI: Sometimes I favor those poems which molt their skins, harden and change to butterflies over long seasons of revision. "Good News! Nilda is Back" was easy to detect and even easier to catch. I wrote it in one day. Its goal was to illuminate and at the same time to preserve the mystery of a woman who works up close, yet lives in a far off recess of her own. It was raining the day I saw the window sign about Nilda, and I wanted a rain dance to enter the poem. I like those Spanish place names. I liked Nilda without knowing her or knowing her news—an affectionate feeling like the memory of my Spanish students, mamitas, bantam warriors armed with Avon products of eternal love and other illusions:

GOOD NEWS! NILDA IS BACK

Good News! Nilda is back,
the sign huzzahs
in the Beauty Shoppe

as the rain combs
the sky over and over
like a grandmother combing
the hair of a child.

Impermanent waves

of rain on the street;
the trees are straight
but the city bends.

Nilda is back
from Guayaquil,
Quito, Ponce, San Jose,

to tease the gringo smiles
of blue-eyed wives
in the raining city.

And now she cha chas
up the aisles
to supervise the upswept lines
of an aging lady

who does not know why Nilda comes
or why she goes
or where her hair uncurls at night
damp at the edge from waves of love.

CH: Your poem "On First Using Purple" is dedicated to Juan Echevarria. I feel I should know who he is. Would you tell me? And who is Queen Tiy? (I often felt in reading your book that a page or two of footnotes, explaining allusions, would have been most helpful. Maybe for a second edition?)

CI: I met Juan Echevarria, a 35-year-old cane cutter from central Puerto Rico in a welfare program for illiterates. After the "my name is" introduction came the "how to hold a pencil" lesson. Perhaps because I didn't like pencils, their gray emanations, I soon began to pass around Crayola crayons much to the delight of my students, most of whom had never applied color to anything except, maybe, to a wall. Echevarria always asked for the purple crayon and later made purple sketches of palm trees, birds and the mountains of his home.

Queen Tiy was the mother of Iknaton (Amenhotep IV), first recorded monotheist, husband of Nefertiti, defier of the ruling priesthood in Egypt, circa 1,370 B.C. Actually, I didn't know most of this, but one night several years ago I dreamed that I was searching for the cities of "Tiy" and "Holafarnes." The dream spelled these places for me clearly so I knew that "Tiy" was not "tea" or "tee." Intrigued, I checked it out, discovered Tiy, and rediscovered the world of Thebes. Holafarnes remains a puzzle although it might suggest my father—"holy farness?" Amen.

CH: Your two Space Cage Poems continue to fascinate me though I'm not sure I'm totally at home in them yet. Could you provide some introductory commentary for those two poems?

CI: Would it have helped, I wonder, if I'd named the poems "Space *John* Cage I and II?" Probably not. Although he's the Cage that jailed the words. Well, to be specific, neither John Cage nor his words, but rather the white spaces scattered like rectangles of snow through his first book, *Silences*, prompted the poems. On page 212 there's a long vertical space like an elevator shaft. My compulsion was to fill the emptiness, to mark the bare walls with secret graffiti. The date of the first Space Cage poem was 2/22/68 and I wrote directly in that book: "I want to centipede this space with dark footsteps ..." Started the next day, the second Space Cage was influenced by snow and one of Cage's phrases, "no to all our questions" which I spun around to, "snow to all our answers." Incidentally, I'm currently defacing Ferlinghetti's *Backwards to Far Places*, which has about 50 page-size spaces, one for each of his poems.

CH: A *New York Times* reviewer spoke of your "adventuresomeness" in contrast to the "flat, cool tone" that so typifies much of contemporary poetry. Do you too share in the impatience the reviewer clearly feels with much of current, modish poetry?

CI: No, I try to treat most of the poems I read with patience and respect. Besides, I'm a born eclectic. It seems to me that there are walking poets and dancing poets and poets that are both. By dancing I mean strongly cadenced music—Roethke's "My Papa's Waltz." By walking I mean a more subtle motion hovering close to prose but still poetry. Galway Kinnell is a Fred Astaire. Mona Van Duyn is a Cyd Charisse and Yeats was a Nijinsky. David Ignatow is an eloquent and thoughtful walker. Robert Creeley gets there quickly and never takes an adjective to lunch. Of course, if you're asking me whether I'd like a dancer or walker with me on a deserted island, my answer is Gene Kelly.

CH: *The Woman Who Loved Worms* is your first book and collects poems from about a ten-year period. Would you talk about some of the problems of ordering, structuring a whole book of poems?

CI: Poems aren't usually written for collections, but collections are assembled for readers (God willing). The Chop Suey approach homogenizes all flavors, but I suppose it sometimes works if the ingredients are prime. To answer your question, there's thematic order and chronological order, pacing, size and mood. A whole clutch of somber poems or too many lengthy ones can make a dreary omelet. I arranged the first third of my book in biographical order starting with the collar my father removed to make me come true. Then came other sections, each characterized by love, fantasy, city life, etc. Each segment was named by an appropriate word taken from one of the poems in the group.

CH: A favorite topic of poets seems to be "dry spells." Do you ever go for long periods when you don't write? How do you survive during them (if you have them), what do you do to get out of them?

CI: Sure, I have my droughts and floods plus a lot of neutral weather. "Spooling," my method for unwinding words without thought to content or punctuation, sometimes helps. Baffling and attractive phrases may appear on the third or fourth page of a spool and can be a springboard to a poem. Stripteasing a word can be diverting. For example: Change, Chang, Chan, cha cha, ha, a. Also reading translations. Try Paul Celan, Vasko Popa, or the enlightened Penguin Book publishers who give you French, Spanish, Japanese, German and Italian poets from the early centuries to modern times. Remember what Cervantes said: "Patience, and shuffle the cards."

CH: If you were asked to choose one poem that you didn't write (one already written) but that you wish you had, what poem would it be, and why?

CI: If you want me to choose, I'll opt for the monumental. Dante's *Divine Comedy* because of its drama, music, magnificence, because of its complex structures, symbols, 100 cantos representing the perfection of the number 100, the dark forest of error, Hell and in nine circles of crime, purgatory and its penitents moving in flame to be purged, paradise of nine spheres containing mystic powers of the stars. And this from a collapsed Catholic.

CH: Are you reading any books now (not books of poetry) that you care to recommend to our readers?

CI: Yes. For a journey into outer space try *Worlds in Collision* by Immanuel Velikovsky—news of an unstable solar system and a theory of catastrophe in our planet's early history caused by Venus being wrenched from Jupiter. For a detour into inner space, try the undeservedly obscure Antonio Porchia (1886–1968). His book of aphorisms, *Voices*, translated by W.S. Merwin, was published by Big Table, Chicago, Illinois, 1969. Here are some examples of his work: "Man goes nowhere. Everything comes to man like the morning," and "It is less degrading to fear than to be feared." Then there's the fierce Ambrose Bierce, American misanthrope (1842–1913). Sample his *Devil's Dictionary* for such definitions as: "Wedding, n., a ceremony at which two persons undertake to become one, one undertakes to become nothing, and nothing undertakes to become supportable." And while you're at it, look to the spider. I recently picked up a copy of *Spiders and Their Kin*. Who knows what poetry might spin from the Coelotes spider who summons her young to share the food, stamps her fourth leg to warn them of danger and gets eaten by them when she dies.

CH: Do you see your poems, the ones yet to be written, the ones you'll be writing in the next five or ten years, as going any particular direction? Do you sense a pattern forming?

CI: I'll be damned if I know where my poetry's going. But I'm open to adventures.

Jim Gorman

"The Power of Words"

Parnassus: Poetry in Review, 7.1, 1978

JIM GORMAN: I've heard that when you were in the fifth grade, two girls laughed at your recitation of a Kipling poem. Is that true? What did you do?

CI: Kipling? I can't remember, but it was a poem. I sometimes think that Robert Frost's counsel to the young poet, that he go into this world with a "tough snout for punishment," must hark back to one or more detractors in his childhood—a thick-skinned heckler in the school yard, a bully from the right side of the tracks. My hecklers were a duo of grim-faced sisters in long-ago Cleveland—when I was ten. I still recall with a sharp twinge of humiliation that I recited a poem to them with all the lilt I could muster. "Lah de dah" they sang, the notes burning in my ear as I ran home. Wrongly or not, I trace to that time my vow of many years to keep mum about my poetry. It wasn't until my senior year in high school, and then with trepidation, that I brought my poems out of the closet and into the living rooms of a few dimly comprehending but sympathetic friends.

JG: How old were you when you first went "into the closet" to write poems?

CI: Twelve. My first poem (and it wasn't written in the closet) was an onomatopoeic ode to the jangle of milk bottles deposited at dawn in the city streets. What spurred me to set the words and music down with an eye towards stanzas and a steadfast left-hand margin, I no longer remember, but the excitement of writing it, of making something palpable out of those dumb, insomniacal, small hours of the morning still reverberates, if dimly, in my mind.

JG: Then it was life around you, experience, not literary models that started you writing poems?

CI: Yes and no. There were also literary models, most of them oral, at least until I came to America. Catechisms, psalms, droning chants, the literature of rosary beads, a whole litany of saints' lives, and Christ's parables were the stories of my childhood. Although the words in French or vulgate Latin are mostly lost in the cells of my memory bank, the rhythm and chimes of the language persist in my love for alternating lines of heavy and light syncopation, the tones and consonants and vowels. Later, when I came to America, I found in the basement of my foster home a dozen or more frayed, clothbound books: Zane Grey cowboy potboilers, *Anthony Adverse*, the Bible. *That's* when I discovered Rudyard Kipling. I was no more than ten when I started to learn "Gunga Din" by heart. What "bhisti" meant or "juldee," I had no idea. As a matter of fact, I read the poem in a cloud of incomprehension. But how I basked in the sounds, the muscular swagger of "you limping lump of brick dust." And then there was the steamy glamor of "Mandalay," another poem I committed to memory, letting my tongue wrap around those pure rhymes and Burmese words, the trochaic beat of the lines, Kipling's grand hoot and roar coming out of a time more confident than ours. That lure of palm trees and dawns out of China, the attraction to the far off and strange hasn't yet abandoned me, and though I write my portion of downhome-in-the-gutter poems. The exotic, like a dish of glistening mango, does more to heighten my senses than any plain potato. But I have to be on guard against those seducers: the satin-ruby words, the artificial peacocks in their glittering and pompous strut.

JG: You mention your coming to America. What problems—other than the two grim-faced sisters—did you have adjusting to American society?

CI: I arrived, a spirited child of eight, and apart from the usual, small needling aimed at an alien presence by peers, I don't recall great hardships integrating into the street life and school life of my new neighborhood. At home, there was some ambivalence about my presence, which had been arranged as a way of cementing my foster parents' flawed and boozy marriage. Perhaps that's why there were so many curt reprimands at my failing to interpret English instructions, and mutterings about the "frog" in the household. Perhaps, too, that's the reason English became so important to learn and cultivate as a barricade against hostility. It was a lifeboat. I'm not sure if my early, eager mastery of English held in it the chromosomes of the poet-to-be, but it's interesting to speculate whether language as a survival mechanism could be a common prelude to poetry.

JG: And you were "the frog"?

CI: Oh yes. Green and foreign. And I still am to a certain extent.

JG: What about your writing habits? Do you write every day?

CI: Doing things at a set time has always been anathema to me. I would have made a rotten soldier, a "klutzy" surgeon. But I do get around to writing at least once a day, invariably in the afternoon or early evening. I have never done anything memorable before noon. The writing I get to may be correspondence (I enjoy writing and receiving letters), journal entries, or revisions of poems. I always seem to have a larger backlog of poems than I have time, and this might be the result of not having a writing regimen to click my heels to every day.

JG: How do your poems begin?

CI: Often, with a line that ricochets in my head and then waits patiently for an association to form around it. Or something may ignite from a line I've eavesdropped on, "found poetry" on walls, newspapers. Even a wine list can set my head spinning. I like fooling around with first drafts of poems in restaurants; that glazed feeling of well-being that comes from being served and dining well can stir me into poetry. Recently, for example, a stream of rose and castle images poured out of a menu that listed Chateau La Rose Trintaudon as a recommended wine.

JG: When something new begins, say in the middle of a restaurant, what do you do?

CI: Frequently, I scrawl down lines in a notepad I tote in my purse. I try to carry it everywhere. It also serves as a recorder of street signs, literary graffiti (re-reading a 1957 journal, I see that I copied "Who's Afraid of Virginia Wolf" from a toilet door at Chumley's in Greenwich Village—this several years before Albee's play), snippets of overheard conversation, and museum lore. For instance, the latest dope on planetary days (Jupiter's is ten hours long), or the names of the guests at a zebra kill in the Serengeti Plain (blackbacked jackal, Ruppell's griffin, maribou storks, etc.). If I get a poem sketched out in my mini-notebook, I often transfer it to an 8 x 11 yellow, lined pad and work on it sheet by sheet. I've gotten into the habit of letting a poem cool its heels when it (or I) gets overheated with too many metaphors or satin-ruby words. Typing up the first draft, a task I tend to put off as long as I can, forces me to jettison self-indulgent phrases and to face the poem with more detachment.

As the poem progresses I institute a kind of staple-paper-date system, taking the original line or stanza from the back of an envelope, a scrap of paper—I'm not teutonic in my work habits, but neither am I slipshod—and stapling it to a revised draft #1. This draft is then dated and added onto until I get the thing right. When the poem is ready for sending out, it goes into a blue labeled folder. If the file becomes too bulky, I thin it out, leaving only the major revisions in the poem's dossier. An average poem is probably whipped into shape over a period of six to eight weeks, but some of my autobiographical work requires more time to steep. "Meeting in London," and "Priest, My Father, Priest" (from *The Woman Who Loved Worms*), for example, evolved over a span of several years. Sometimes I imagine myself as a lifeguard to my drowning poems, trying to rescue them from the limitations of my wit and inspiration. Anyway, I hold onto what I have, no matter how faltering, believing Mr. Micawber's maxim that "something will turn up." More often than not, it does if I prepare myself to wait it out for a time when there is resonance between me and the poem.

JG: What if that time of resonance doesn't come?

CI: Well, then I'm like an obstinate carpenter. I get it right by constant tinkering.

JG: Do you hold onto everything? Are you that obstinate? Or can you throw out your "artificial peacocks," as you called them earlier?

CI: Yes, I think so. There's always a place in my current journal for lists of what I call "beautiful discards." Of course, the discards are rarely "beautiful," but the word serves to soften the blow of eviction. Last November, waiting for my husband at the Rainbow Room, atop the R.C.A. building, I scratched down these lines in my notepad: "Darius, nix/ on your onyx, diabase, gneiss,/ New York New York outwits/ your store of pleasure,/ Persepolis, bah!" Now maybe I can inflate that ditty into something neighboring on poetry, but as the thing sits in my journal, it's doggerel, high-class, not embarrassing enough to be chucked out, but too unpromising for placement in my unmarked file (a folder of poems in a near state of ripening). Another ruse I use for prodding myself into poems is to shoplift words. Stealing a writer's phrase is plagiarism, but filching his or her words is perfectly kosher. A.R. Ammons has a rich mine of words for excavation: salient, continuum, peripheral, motion—a quasi-scientific and sometimes latinate diction. Dylan Thomas leans towards sonorous compounds: seashaken, dogdayed, beasthood, cockcrow, dark-vowelled, windfall, mousehole. For word-heisting, I especially like the *New York Times* literary section. Last week, for instance, it gave up the following delectables: dole, fiasco, doyens (of), scoop, citadel, gerbil, unhurried, and hansom (as in hansom cab). Like a collage artist or a "literary jackdaw" (as a friend once described me), I pluck out the words I might need to make a glinting line, or barring the good luck of pouncing on the right word, I please myself by rereading them for the joy of their sounds, meanings and shades of meanings, their very look on the page.

JG: Then your love for exotic sounds, for your "dish of glistening mango" does not begin and end with Kipling?

CI: Oh no. And not just exotic sounds. I repeat, meanings and shades of meanings, and the look of a word on a blank page can excite me as much as the sound. I find words everywhere. I love the dictionary, but also trusty *Roget's*. I remember reading that Sylvia Plath dandled the thesaurus on her lap while writing out first drafts. I also own a set of *Life* magazine nature books on primates, early man, the universe, the poles (Arctic and Antarctic), ecology, the sea, and an almost complete series of Golden Nature guidebooks on wildflowers, insects, spiders, seashells and trees of eastern North America.

JG: Robert Creeley talks about having a "shed" behind his house where he goes when he has to write—to get away from his family, the ringing phone. What is your work area like? You live in Manhattan, in an apartment—what do you use, besides restaurants, as a get-away shed?

CI: The Japanese have a term for the writer's shed away from home. They call it *kanzume* or "tin can." William Jay Smith has risked and won a wonderfully long, loose-lined poem of the same name ("The Tin Can") which begins: "I have gone into the tin can: not in the late spring fleeing a/stewing, meat and fish smelling city of paper houses...." My "tin can" sits in an area intended as a dining room—a small, slightly elevated rectangle of space that overlooks a city courtyard boasting five Trees of Heaven and as many dogs. Among them is a German shepherd that howls in counterpoint to my electric typewriter. Why don't they send German Shepherds back to Germany? Sometimes all the hounds of 87th Street set up a chain of yelps when the fire engines roar uptown. But quiet hours reside in New York and I do what I can to use them well. There is no get-away shed except what four-walled solitude I construct in my mind. I've schooled myself to jot down poems almost anywhere, in restaurants of course, but also in the subway, the back of the bus (there's excitement in writing while riding in a hurtle through time that's out of my control), or on a city park bench or through those myriad occasions of waiting that most people, and women in particular, are heir to.

JG: Was your early poetry (before your first book) more formalistic? Do you think it is necessary to first master form in order to break out of it?

CI: I don't know if it's necessary, but I think it's good for the artist to learn the rules he or she is going to break. Most of my early poems, the ones before *The Woman Who Loved Worms,* were written in meter and rhyme. I liked the safety belt of a tight structure, the predictable and orderly machine of echoing rhymes, and I was hooked on the quatrain—a legacy from Emily Dickinson, no doubt. In an obsession for tidy patterns, I even messed around with syllabic verse in total ignorance of haikus, tankas, cinquains or the works of Marianne Moore. My love affair with rhyme, slant and off, pure and internal, approximate and assonantal, remains intact but I'm now more confident, more loose-limbed in the dance of the longer free-verse line. But if I can let a rhymed couplet clinch the last two lines of a poem, if that feels right and inevitable, then it's like a gift to me or to the child in me entranced with the heartbeat of marked-out time.

JG: The "longer free-verse line"? Are your lines getting longer?

CI: I don't know. Deciding the length of a line is sometimes a dilemma. But there are considerations I take into account. One is, how the poem looks. I'm an enemy of the long, scraggly line which is tagged by a two-word line and then proceeds like a sidewinder to zigzag all over the page. Of course, if the poet is a virtuoso with a bag of glittering tricks, I'll go along with, or even relish the shenanigans. I enjoy breaking a line to create suspense, or to lure the reader to expect something and then mildly startle him into another mindset. I tried for that effect in a line from "Leider for a Chocolate Cake" (in my new book): "Eva taking shots/of edelweiss in bloom." In some of the poems completed recently and in the new book, I've sensed a need to ripple a line way out to the edge of the page, as if I wanted to escape the confines of an 8 x 11 cage. I don't know why. An enlarging ego? Yes, maybe, but also a hunger to cover the page with my track marks, to do aggressive battle with empty space. But these, at best, are educated guesses.

JG: You rely a great deal on puns and wordplay. Have you been influenced by the metaphysical poets?

CI: I reveled in wordplay, word games, and riddles long before I knew what "metaphysical" meant, before I'd done (Donne) any reading of the poets linked together under that heading. Why the predilection? I don't exactly know but I did understand early on the power of words and how they can control what you do and who you are. French, in a sing-song Walloon (Belgian) intonation, was my mother tongue, but easily one-half of the wards at the Children's Home spoke Flemish. Incidentally, they were forbidden Flemish much in the same way that American Indian children were once denied their native language in government schools. At any rate, I spent my early years with an ear leaning in on two languages. Beyond a babbling "hello" and "goodbye," I spoke no English when I arrived in the United States at the age of eight, but I had a parrot's flair for mimicry, a quick ear, and learned with impressive speed to deliver more English sentences than I could receive. And I was thrown pronto into the English speaking pool (my foster family spoke no French) where I learned not only to swim, but to float, to turn, and kick almost as if I'd been born in that water. Until the age of fourteen, I retained a trace of my French-speaking origins, a "th/t, f/d" problem that led me to pronounce "three" as "free," "thief" as "fief" and "them" as "dem." That's the way they talk in Brooklyn, someone assured me. Still, I wasn't satisfied and dutifully practiced the tongue-tipping "th" in front of a hand-mirror for months until the blemish was corrected.

JG: What about your poems already in print? Do you still have urges to revise them? What would you do differently about your new book now? Have you considered changes in any of the poems? Or their arrangement?

CI: When Simenon sent his early manuscripts to *the* Colette for comment, she returned them with a hastily penned "too literary, my dear friend." I'm not comparing myself to the estimable creator of Maigret, but my introduction to *The Woman Who Loved Worms,* an essay my editors at Doubleday exhorted me to write, definitely falls in the slot of arty composition, and if I had a second chance, I'd yank the thing out like a superfluous tooth. I'm too close to the pores of *Alive and Taking Names* to see the whole of its imperfections. A few years hence I'll surely wish some poems had been dumped or I'll want to fuss with poems that seemed quite adequate when they entered the collection. Normally, I try to squelch the temptation to tamper with a work once it's in print. There's always too large a stockpile of promising starts to be finished.

JG: All right, then, without tampering, let's talk about *Alive and Taking Names.* I find there are poems in the book which continue to deal with the same subjects as in your first book—your odd parentage, your early upbringing in an orphanage, your search for your mother. I think your poems about these subjects have matured (I am comparing an early poem like "Meeting in London" with "Marthe, the Mar, la Mer, La Mère ..." or "Crucial Stew"). Has time enabled you to gain a better perspective on these subjects?

CI: Each profession has its lexicon, and for our purposes I'll borrow from the vocabulary of the behavioral sciences. The word "process," a condition of movement, but not necessarily progress. But I suppose, without bogging down in existential philosophy, change is neither good nor bad, it happens as a condition of life. My process? A kind of repeated exploration of the void: the parents that weren't, the rearing that had no foothold in bloodlines or genes. Have these poems which focus in on motherhood (and the foreclosing on it) matured? I can't say. Both "Meeting in London" and "Crucial Stew" mark the beginning and end of a process—my birth, my search for my mother. "Meeting in London" starts with a condemnation of her and "Crucial Stew" announces a farewell to illusions. But does this shifting point of view mark an advance? All I recognize is motion—process—and the arrival at another station on a route whose direction is often guided by my need to reconcile the past from where I now stand. Surely, it's easier to master a more challenging and painful task with some isolation from the first hurt. Time is the absolver, the trustiest insulation. I write about abandonment and abortion with some confidence that now the peril which they held is less ingrained in the words that express them. I am safer, feel safer, and when the word is divorced from the imminent reality, it becomes easier to conjure with. Does this make for a more effective poem? You decide.

JG: In "The Sky is an English Priest Undoing His Coat," you tell the story of your conception from your father's point of view. Does this also indicate a mellowing of your attitude toward him as well as your mother?

CI: I sometimes think of autobiographical poetry as "tamed dreams." The nightmarish vision of a slaughtered parent, the mayhem that the nighttime unconscious looses, is defused in the poem to make the message more sane, literate, less savage. To be honest, I still tap a reservoir of both pity and rage—toward both parents. But the wordscape might be deceptive. I think I have mellowed somewhat, and am letting go of the indictment. But meanwhile, I've found a more satisfying way of handling this material. In this case, it's defrocking my father, peeling away his pretense and dignity, and charging him with loss of faith. Of course, there's ambivalence in my accusation. The poem orchestrates old and new feelings. The old rut of pain and a newer compassion.

JG: In the title poem of the new book, "Alive and Taking Names," you are making a kind of pronouncement to the world—that you have arrived at a certain level of maturity and self-awareness. Is the placement of this poem (at the end of the childhood section of the book, Part 1) important?

CI: Tactical might be a better word, but you're right. My works about childhood, I see in reflection, have an inwardness that often excludes what comes with emotional and intellectual growth—a recognition of the outside world, the catalog of its paraphernalia, and, for the purposes of this poem, a listing of its ills and pitfalls. Actually, "Alive and Taking Names" began as a "what if" poem, and a paean to the magical properties of words. For instance, if I were to use the word "grease," would I be "slick," or would the intoning of "plague" make me collapse into disease? A primitive notion, sure enough. For the tally of synonyms, incidentally, I perused my trusty *Roget's*. Again, I was trying to be exotic as well as magical. Whether the poem is a testament to a newfound self-awareness I'm hard put to say. But I notice a feisty, upbeat voice emerging in the lines. I'm not a conscript of *Weltschmerz* or Valium, it seems to say. And rightly so. "Alive and Taking Names" —I admit the title has a slight paranoid twist—becomes not just a poem noting a rite of passage, but a fitting name for the collection itself. Naming things to give them life and direction is one of the things the poet does, albeit with more license than *Webster's*.

JG: You have already talked about your coming to America. I think that one of the unique elements of your new book is its international quality—the voice is that of an American woman, but what she seeks is often not found here. Could you discuss this assessment, especially in relationship to your poems concerning World War II, like "Leider for a Chocolate Cake" and "Home Movie of Poland"?

CI: If by going international I've captured something universal, the trip was worth it. But I'll confess to no conscious awareness that I cast for cosmic truths on other shores. It just seems right that these poems set during a savage time give a dramatic backdrop to an exploration of the human estate. "Home Movie of Poland" largely narrates the loss of my husband's family to the Holocaust, but it is as much concerned with rescue and love. These themes are more abstractly repeated in "Leider for a Chocolate Cake" where the spotlight points not only to Hitler and his cabal, but to the survivors of the firestorm in both a literal and emotional sense. What is central to these poems is the victimization I felt to be my lot as a foster child: unwanted, harassed, often ill used in a house of anti-Semites. I could relate, and did even as a Catholic and later as a blurry Protestant (my foster folks didn't share the faith of my priest-father), to the martyrdom of the Jew. By way of footnote, I converted to reform Judaism fourteen years ago. Anyway, when I flourish my poetry passport for a voyage abroad, it will be, I hope, more than an expedition to dig up artifacts of my alien past. Like any good earthling, I want to take in the adventures of this planet, and to mark my passage as I go.

JG: Your new book also contains several poems about women who are not closely related to you, but seem to have made a deep impression on you. Could you tell me something about the Eskimo woman in "Old Woman, Eskimo," about Deanna Durbin in "Deanna Durbin, Come Home," about the Duchess in "Frocking the Duchess"?

CI: Not related? I wonder. Without belaboring the shopworn thesis about the poet's personae inhabiting his works, I think we can tap Gestalt dream theory to help center these women in my world. The dream, Gestaltists say, projects in all its images parts of the dreamer. A train crossing a trestle at midnight—the engine smoke, the ties and rails, the moon and timbers of the railroad bridge, all are unintegrated parts of the dreamer. Lately I've come to see my "people" poems in these terms, and the women in my new book as aspects of myself still not totally metabolized.

JG: Then, you have never met the Eskimo Woman?

CI: No. Or, only in myself. She is the stoic Inez struggling against real and imaginary odds. Deanna Durbin in her theatrical emanations is a divine *doppelganger* of the adolescent Inez transported to a never-never land of fantasies and dreams. And the Duchess—an imperious and lustful Inez, vain and a trifle fatuous. They come and they go like nomads, these characters who play out parts of my life. I do what I can as an artist to hold them in focus for a moment in the long journey.

JG: The long journey? You sound weary. Is it, and perhaps this is an unfair question from a man, but, is it a longer journey for a woman poet? What about the "concept of 'femaleness'"—your phrase from four years ago. Do you still think maleness and femaleness is "destined to fade" from poetry?

CI: I still believe the "female" experience is culturally, socially, and even organically unique. The man/woman differentiation tends to be fairly strong in the works of either gender. This *may* change, and I'm still hopeful. Not that I look forward to a time of truly androgynous poetry, but rather to an end to that depressing literary chauvinism which often discourages poets from venturing into modes of expression conventionally associated with the opposite sex. Also, I'd like to see, as a way to speed up the process, a broad acceptance of the Russian practice of initialling given names. Poetry by J. Dickey. James? Josephine? Might not this device provide the necessary camouflage to liberate the poet from a fixation on his or her genes?

JG: Has it also been a longer journey for you because you began late? You were almost 40 when you published your first book.

CI: Yes, once in a while I feel remedial, like a dunce in a pointed hat who's been left back in poetry's school. I still confess to little pangs of envy when a "wunderkind" poet hits the celebrity trail at 20. And I'm prone to respect, fairly or not, those poets who've spent an apprenticeship of years in the craft. But in some quirky way, I've been sharpened by early deprivation, by struggling out of the miasma of low self-esteem. Strength comes from testing strength. No one wins a marathon without a stretch of painful miles and hurdles to cross. That I've been the architect of some of my own hurdles hasn't lessened the exertions. And then, too, who cares that Joyce Cary published his first novel, *Aissa Saved* when he was 43, *The Horse's Mouth* at 56. Or that Wallace Stevens sent his early poems to *Poetry,* attaching a wonderfully litotic note: "I am 35 years of age and work for the Hartford Life Insurance Company"? Yeats wrote best in his fifties. John Hall Wheelock was still going strong at ninety. I wouldn't be 20 again for a shipload of diamonds; it's an upbeat state of being, primetime, if you like, to reach the middle forties with a well received book tucked in my belt, another one off the presses, and the contents of a third waiting for assemblage in my files.

Kevin Walzer

"Rallying Cry"

Bridge Magazine 1, 2000

KEVIN WALZER: The autobiographical impulse in your work seems to be your great subject. Certainly *Clemency* appears to address the topic even more than *Family Life*. Do you see this continuing in your work?

COLETTE INEZ: No. *Family Life* was published years before my mother died in 1992. Against her wishes when she was alive—she wanted to keep my birth a secret from her family—I then declared myself to her family and was rewarded by meeting cousin Maurice who invited me to Paris. His bequest was not of money, but what was even more valuable to a writer: a legacy of stories and anecdotes, photographs and letters that gave flesh and coherence to my story. These gifts allowed me to feel more authentic and more visible.

No, I won't assemble another book on the subject, even though I sometimes fantasize my father's San Francisco family seeking me out, sharing their collection of pictures and curios, prompting me to write about my paternal side, a shadowy place in my life. But it won't happen. I don't think a story like mine ever comes to complete resolution; one accepts a state of perpetual but manageable longing.

KW: What else would you describe as claiming your imagination?

CI: Astronomy, a study whose grandeur and mystery speaks to me as a religious surrogate. The communal wine of images pour through our telescope (a Celestron 8) where in childhood they once trickled from a chalice on the altar. I'm also moved by gleanings of other peoples' stories: the death of a contentious neighbor girl transformed into a beauty queen, the intensity of adolescent crushes, prose poems on themes that continue to console me, for instance the world of nature, which I think of as beneficent and democratic. Butterflies, flowers, the chronicle of birds and bees holds my fascination, which some might call an obsession with conception and birth.

KW: Your early work shows the influence of surrealism. *The Woman Who Loved Worms* is an example of this. Your work in the 1980s and 1990s is more relaxed and direct without losing the imagistic power. What accounts for this relaxation?

CI: Might I say that I was reassured by a long and sympathetic marriage that added to my growing self-confidence. I felt increasingly able to sustain a longer work, became attracted to story telling rather than fashioning the quick surreal poems empowered by sundry metaphors. I see from the outpouring of poems published in the seventies that rich intensity and spontaneity beckoned to me more than plain speech and the narrative line. And I also wanted to broaden my possibilities as a poet and to be understood by my readers. Ten years ago I also began sporadically writing a prose memoir and gradually found it easier to hear prose rhythms, to think in longer, more fluid sentences.

KW: As your work has grown more realistic in its scenes, it also seems to have grown denser musically; you show great skill and finesse with the free verse line. Has a rich music always been important to you, or have you concentrated on developing this aspect of your work more recently?

CI: How the poems sounds, the music, has always mattered to me. I always read my poems aloud when composing. I love music and even play the piano, but not dazzlingly so; yet I improvise and have a good ear. Early on I plucked out tunes before learning to read notes. Similarly, I was able to parrot English phrases before understanding the language. Poets whose music moved me in childhood? Walter de la Mare, Hart Crane, Wilfred Owen, King David's Song of Songs, the hymnal music of Emily Dickinson, even the fife and drum of Rudyard Kipling whose thrumming verses I committed to memory before becoming fluent in English.

KW: Describe some of your influences as a poet. Who did you read during your formative days? Your use of line and the striking images bear a resemblance to the stranger, less domestic work of Elizabeth Bishop. Other influences?

CI: I read Bishop and was intrigued by the contrast of her life as a rich orphan to mine as a poor one, but wasn't especially moved by her work which at first I found cold and unavailing. But I've returned to her during the last decade, and newly appreciate the brilliant precision of her portraits.

My early goddesses were the formalists Anne Sexton, Sylvia Plath and Adrienne Rich who gave women of my generation permission to write of bedlam, blood, lust and the body politic, all without mortification. Others? Wallace Stevens. And I also sought out the grand T'ang Dynasty poets: the stately grace of Tu Fu, the profound bitterness of Meng Ciao. More recently I've discovered the Sung Dynasty poet Wu Wen-ying,

a mid-thirteenth century writer of sumptuous language and intricate allusion.
Poetry in translation excites me and I use it in my classes. For example, Chanah and Ari Bloch's translation of Amichai, Nathaniel Tarn and Stephen Mitchell's version of Neruda, the great Spanish poets Garcia Lorca, Machado, Miguel Hernandez, Japanese love poems translated by Sam Hamill, Coleman Bark's *Rumi*, etcetera.

KW: Would you describe yourself as more of a lyric or a narrative poet? Or do those terms have any meaning for your work?

CI: Both. I would hope I tell stories lyrically, or I write lyric poetry with a scaffolding of the story. Those kinds of definitions don't interest me.

KW: You have made your living for the past two decades as a university teacher, as many poets do. How does teaching balance with the writing?

CI: While I juggle part-time teaching with private students, public readings, fitful contest judging, writing reviews, blurbs and book introductions, the brain drain of teaching isn't something I bellyache about. I lead a privileged life and sometimes pinch myself at the windfall, not of money, but of the real wealth the life of poetry affords us.

Students sometimes inspire my work. One, a Kashmiri in a Columbia MFA program, introduced me to the *classical* Arabic ghazal; I'd been acquainted with Adrienne Rich's looser versions of the form from her translation of Ghalib. Another student has me exploring the rousing and fearless Gaelic poems of Nuala Ni Dhomhnaill.

KW: Describe a typical writing day.

CI: I rise a bit before ten (having already said I haven't done or written anything memorable before noon), make a mug of decaf, jot down an entry in my journal—though not every day—switch on the computer, shuffle papers, check my plan book and "must-do" list, and work on poems. I'm a chronic reviser, except on those rare occasions when I'm visited by the God of the Ceiling who flings a poem on the page before I print it up.

The letters-to-be answered file is opened and I brew another mug of coffee, followed by some dilly-dallying before tackling a larger project, a book review, and perhaps a blurb, all projects I tend to face with twitching angst. I work on and off until one, call my husband for news about his free-lance morning, get dressed, forage in the refrigerator for lunch fixings, sometimes visit the neighborhood bakery-restaurant for quiche and salad, read *The New York Times*, empty my lobby mailbox and answer letters demanding immediate response. In good weather, I trek through Central Park and, depending on my schedule, will or won't return to my word processor once back home to work through the afternoon.

KW: In other interviews you have described a growing audience for poetry. Can you elaborate on this observation?

CI: I believe there's a large untapped audience for poetry of all stripes—best of all, well read poetry with welcoming introductions that engagingly give hints about the poems' origins, composition and other anecdotal material. Not poetry of the android bloodless school, but skillfully written work with wit and pulse, that's what I want to hear. On the wider scene, competitive slam poetry is grabbing headlines, as is thumpingly high-spirited Cowboy poetry of the "get along little doggerel" school.

And then I hear the West Coast rappers are engaged in a feud with the East Coast rappers (which student friends tell me are superior). Bookstore readings are also burgeoning. Poetry flourishes, admittedly with more writers than readers, but a heady mix of word-love is at large in the land; it's exhilarating stuff.

KW: Does poetry have a place outside of a university setting?

CI: Poetry may or may not be the oldest profession, but surely it will endure as long as there are troubadours, myth makers, lovers and worlds we choose to interpret, celebrate, vilify or mourn. Consciousness of our presence on this minuscule third planet from the sun, circling in the exurbs of our galaxy, requires that poetry makes itself manifested, and I consider myself someone who sends out a rallying cry.

Kevin Bezner

The Way Home: A Conversation with Colette Inez

This interview has its roots in one conducted publicly on April 15, 1997 as part of the Spring Literary Festival at Central Piedmont Community College in Charlotte, North Carolina. A version Bezner edited from a tape of that initial interview was published in *Main Street Rag*, volume 5, number 2, summer, 2000. In 2001, Inez supplied answers to additional questions posed by Bezner and revised her earlier answers.

KB: You've drawn on your Catholic upbringing to write poems like "A Faithful Likeness," which seems almost a prayer to Saint Francis. You certainly are a spiritual person. But are you a religious person? Did the history of your parents and your upbringing as a Catholic turn you away from religion?

CI: Liturgy is not my strong suit, although as a collapsed Catholic I'm drawn to the ceremonies of the Church, the theater of incense and incantations, of Holy Communion. Married to a secular Jew whose Yeshiva education soured him on theology, I can describe myself on good days as a hedonistic, skeptic pagan; the notion of many gods is so much livelier than that of one Supreme Being. Better The Supremes? And on bad days, I'm a half-hearted nihilist, a lethargic anarchist. What dazzles me is the mystery inherent in large, unanswerable questions: Who are we? Where did we come from? Why are we here? These enigmas continue to fascinate me.

Yes, no doubt, the history of my parents whose fate was manipulated by the rigid laws of the Roman Catholic Church turned me away from its assumed consolations.

KB: You say in "A Quarrel Put to Rest" that you wanted to run off to sea. What did the sea mean to you as a child, and what does it mean for you now?

CI: As a child, my sea was a frozen lake when I skated with other fledglings at the institute, and it was the blue on the map our Sisters rolled down in geography class. My first look at the ocean was beyond the rail of a ship sailing from Antwerp to England just before World War II. I remember being afraid of demons that swam below us, but I also loved the sea's immensity and the promise it gave of delivering me into what I thought would be the hands of my true parents. Yes, I wanted to be a sailor, to knot lanyards and dance the hornpipe—scrubbing decks was not part of the picture—and I still remember the pang of disappointment when I learned girls could not go to sea. In those days gender specific was not a household phrase.

KB: The poem "Orphans of All Denominations Will Meet," which opens your book *Getting Under Way*, came from a sign on the subway?

CI: New York City is full of surreal images like the sign on the wall of the 96th Street subway station, which read "Orphans of all denominations will meet in Central Park," an odd instruction that I copied in a small notepad I usually carry with me. Soon after I felt the agitation that comes before a poem. This particular poem spoke to a number of my interests: a love of place names, in this case riddled with "do not" signs, and religious language. I relate the orphan's life with "Shalt nots" harking back to the Old Testament, although my childhood in the New Testament prevailed. I was brought to a Belgian orphanage at ten days of age and released nearly eight years later by the Sisters who ran it.

KB: There's a great contrast between that poem and the one that follows it in *Getting Under Way*, "The Collar around My Thoughts," where you confront the idea of your father, a priest, taking off his collar to have intercourse with your mother.

CI: This poem was inspired in a theater while I was seated behind a priest. I had known for some years that my father was a Roman Catholic priest ordained the year I was born. Staring at the priest's collar, I felt a tightening around my neck, and in a leap of association pictured my birth father snapping off his collar before I was conceived. My father remains a puzzle to me. His family never answered my letters to them, likely to keep intact the myth of their celibate and celebrated man of the cloth. The mystery of the God-like eminence who made me is the source of a persistent obsession. But while I was born and reared in Brussels, I choose to place my origins in Paris, where I was made to come true.

KB: How did you find out about your parents? When did you first learn of this story?

CI: After World War II, I discovered to my astonishment that I was not a U.S. citizen. My foster parents in Merrick, Long Island, had not registered me as foreign born, which meant on technical grounds I was subject to deportation, leading to various encounters with immigration. Quite by chance, I located the name of the lawyer who arranged my coming to America, and seated with him inside his car, outside of a bingo parlor in Richmond, Virginia, he identified my blood father: not by name, but as a priest, and confided the even more exciting news that my mother was alive. A clue to this reality had earlier been dropped by my foster parents, who I was told took me in the hope of mending their frayed marriage. They were wedded to Jim Beam, to booze, and when drunk claimed, "You're the bastard of a nun and a priest." They were half right.

KB: You never really developed a relationship with your father, right?

CI: Sadly, I never knew him. He died of a heart attack at 48 when I believe I was four. My mother since told me of his visit to the orphanage in civilian clothes when I was likely a toddler.

KB: What kind of relationship did you have with your mother?

CI: I didn't have a relationship with her until a voyage of discovery through Europe at age 20. My search took me to her lodgings in Oxford, England, where she researched Church history for local dons. I had intruded on her circumspect life, on a reclusive and withdrawn woman who hid her indiscretion and our history from her family. She insisted that we preserve the secret and would allow us to correspond but without any written reference to our true relationship. I was grateful for that qualified permission. To her credit, after about 10 years of sharing bland weather reports, she agreed to answer some personal questions. What did I ask? "Did you love my father?" No, she wrote, she was in awe of him, an Aristotle scholar of some repute. "Why did you place me with the Sisters?" So you would grow up to be a good Catholic.

Following our first meeting in 1953, our relationship remained sparse and thin. My mother left England to return to her birthplace in France (Nérac in Gascony) where joined by my husband, Saul, I visited her twice. The last visit was in 1986 after the death of her only sister, whom I had once met as Marthe's "American friend." My aunt Jeanne never learned of our mother-daughter bond. In my mother's presence, I played my assigned role of the invisible daughter, our conversation punctuated with mundane comments—"It's warm for May"; "Have you seen the local ruins?"

KB: Did you see or feel that as a rejection?

CI: Yes, but I have come to let go of the indictment. Here was an extraordinarily private person threatened by an intruder, a stranger. So she must have felt. Of course, I yearned that she throw her arms around me and say, "My brave daughter, I want to introduce you to your family."

KB: How did you discover your parents as subject?

CI: I came late to poetry, and it never occurred to me that one could write about one's life. That's why I'm so grateful to Sexton and Plath, who gave women like me license to write about our passions and grievances.

KB: I'm glad you brought up Plath. It's striking how many of the poems in *Getting Under Way* either use the German language or have a sound similar to that which Plath was able to so wonderfully get into her poetry. Why Nazis? Why German? Is there a Plath connection, a greater connection?

CI: Plath is part of it. People ask me if I lived through the European war. Actually, no, I escaped before the occupation, but the war *was* very close to me, and I worried about my schoolmates, my Belgian friends in the hands of the Nazis. And, of course, there was fear and hatred in my work—as Plath had in great amounts—of Nazis, of oppression. In my case, as an abused child, I could identify with the metaphor of the persecuted Jew.

KB: You're able to get that history of your having been abused and rejected as an illegitimate child into your poems, but at the same time this isn't your only concern. What are you doing in writing your poems that enables you to take your subjects elsewhere?

CI: At work is a certain distancing that one learns through practice. I try hard to avoid the great pitfall of autobiographical or confessional writing: self-pity. I make an effort to achieve a certain detachment, especially from those who have harmed me. Poets need not be fierce, avenging angels to speak out with authenticity and power. I dislike the word "forgiveness," and prefer "understanding." To understand the motives and shortfalls of others is a strength, I suppose. I do believe one should hang in there and endure.

KB: So many of your poems have something to do with photographs or paintings. Why is that?

CI: During my first eight years at the institute, it was the rule of nuns to forbid the use of mirrors. "Beauty is empty," they would say, or "vanity distracts from piety." This deprivation only aroused curiosity that for me was satisfied when first seeing my reflected face at the bottom of a milk mug. It was clear to me that the image was no visitation, and as a sensual child—all children are sensual—I was hungry for more encounters. Beyond this, I came to recognize likenesses between my other friends at the orphanage and relatives who visited them: similar hairlines, tones of voice, gestures. I saw those resemblances and wondered about my own family. For a while I imagined a "twin sister" mirrored in the mug, saw her in shiny surfaces, puddles and doorknobs, and for a time it was comforting. Yet when I first met my mother and studied her face, I found it differed sharply from mine; hers was long, oval, Mediterranean, with a long nose and slender lips. My looks were clearly from my paternal side—that is, if the only photo of my father I located later on typified his family. Flashing forward a bit, after my mother's death in 1992, my cousin Maurice, pointed out that my left eyebrow resembled that of my mother. I was touched that he saw something of her in me. Yes, photos and paintings are thematic in many of my poems and serve, I suppose, a feast of seeing after the meager fare of my early days.

KB: Your poem on James Ensor is one of your most interesting formally. You use some of his language. You must have researched Ensor. Why Ensor?

CI: Ensor was not only an original artist but an eloquent writer as well, a person who flexed impressive verbal muscles. I came upon his correspondence in *Letters of the Great Artists*, Random House, and recognizing the dates of his birth and death, I realized his penultimate decade of life, and my first, were spent in Belgium, but in contrasting social milieus. While I slurped cabbage soup with wards of the state, Ensor dined with the king of Belgium. That fascinated me, and I started a poem with Ensor's words followed by my own. And with each stanza I found myself transforming, until at the end of the poem I was Ensor's equal, that together we shared the aristocracy of art. The poem underwent many revisions and in the process of tightening, giving it shape, I felt a surge of self-confidence, a self-love, if you will.

KB: Spending time in nature seems to bring you great joy as well. Bees, birds, mayflies, and flowers are all essential elements of your poetry. Was nature one more thing you turned to as a child "hungry for images," as you say?

CI: Birds and bees, is it? It sounds as if I'm interested in procreation and think on some unconscious level I am fixated on the making of me by my parents who then ejected me from the nest. The world of nature, not human nature, hums and buzzes with sexuality, with the excitement and consolations of physical beauty. Like music it seemed to offer me a more perfect world than its human counterpart, but one learns that's a sentimental notion. Life in the forest and sea is just as fierce and cruel as ours. Looking at stars through a telescope or at rotifers under a microscope fills the hunger I have for images, and for a sense of self in an unavailing universe.

KB: Do you have any solitary places in New York that allow you to continue this interest in nature, or must you go outside the city for solace?

CI: On the edge of Turtle Pond in Central Park, there's an overlook for watching a cormorant drying its outstretched wings in the sun, or I can see a cheeky red winged blackbird perched on a wooden post inches from where I stand. Recently, my husband and I gazed with admiration at a snowy egret stalking a minnow in slow motion. The sculpture gallery at the Metropolitan Museum of Art—we live in walking distance of it—serves coffee within a space I can share with the great poet, Sappho, memorialized in stone. Sometimes we take our telescope or giant binoculars to the Delaware River in Pennsylvania and find grandeur in Orion's nursery of blue stars or the Galilean moons of Jupiter.

KB: I'd like to end by asking you some questions that you in a way answer in a poem called "Questions for Discussion." "Questions for Discussion" starts with the question, "To what extent do you love?"

CI: I must tell you that I love to a wide extent my husband, Saul, who has been an important source of equilibrium and joy to me. We're a devoted pair whose 37-year marriage was celebrated on July 26, 2001.

KB: How do you justify kisses?

CI: With kisses. Kisses. Kisses.

KB: What omissions are most important?

CI: The omission of lifelong revenge. The omission of rancor. To be rancorous all one's life over injuries is to wound oneself as an artist.

Essays

Sharon Klander

Worlds Made with Words: The Poetry of Colette Inez

I first met Colette Inez in 1990 when she was a guest writer at Ohio University and I was a Ph.D. candidate working on a creative dissertation of poems. More than a decade later, I still go back to her written comments regarding my first manuscript, including her impressions of the first section "with its family history interwoven with the rituals of the Catholic Church, the setting of Gulf Coast Texas." It's little wonder that Inez would take particular note in my work of setting, family, and church ritual, considering her own childhood and family history—given up as an infant for adoption by her French, medieval-scholar mother, who was not married to Inez's father, an American, Roman Catholic priest, and subsequent experiences in abusive foster homes—all well-documented not only in interviews and autobiographies but, of course, given the greatest depth of expression in her poems. Here one clearly sees a pointed interest in naming and controlling space from a woman for whom, as an abandoned, bastard child in a dogmatic, patriarchal, even liturgical society, the power to name was lost at the most basic level of self-identity. Further, the loss of control of space for young Colette often meant the inability to control even the space of own body, a typical circumstance of abused children. Therefore, one sees again and again in Inez's poems the use of language to create small worlds both of and outside her own body in which she can regain the power of naming—first, in simple identification, through the trope of synecdoche, of objects that stand in for larger realities, and vice versa; and moving, logically, to the outright reclamation of the power of language alone, without juxtaposition's filters, to make and re-make the worlds in which she and those she loves move and have their being.

An early example of synecdoche is found in "A Collar Rounds My Thoughts," in which Inez invests the clerical collar she assumes is worn by the father (in blood, not in faith) she was never allowed to know with the power first to kill by choking, rendering her speechless:

> Priest, my father, priest,
> your collar cuts my neck,
> my resonating breath's
> intake.... (5)

Notice how the act of cloistering or closing off is accomplished by the repetition of the word, "priest," which stands as guard at the front and back doors to the intimate "my father," as if to insure that nothing is let out, nothing is let in—especially not a vow-busting child. In fact, in her placement of this word, Inez indicates its use as synecdoche for the entire Roman Catholic Church and confirms its ability to control the space around the human—the human father as well as his human daughter.

From this beginning, the collar progresses to control a realm more cerebral, including a first connection to the natural world:

> Priest, my father, priest,
> your collar rounds my thought
> like a moon, refractory and white. (5)

Even as Inez allows this symbol of a patriarchal priesthood to bind her thoughts, she immediately undercuts that boundary with a simile that points to a power traditionally feminine—indeed, to a power that, as the Moon goddess, could boast her own priestesses (for example, in the Sumerian culture). In effect, Inez is able to both acknowledge the power of her father and, by extension, the Roman Catholic Church, and to invoke the power of the feminine.

Finally, Inez extends the collar to encompass her entire world:

> Priest, my father, priest,
> your collar rounds my world
> like an equator
> burning to know your life
> interred forever in that faith
> which primed your guilt. (6)

Here, following the now-familiar litany of the first line, Inez recasts the idea of faith, moving away from St. Paul's definition—"the substance of things hoped for, the evidence of things not seen"—a definition wholly appropriate to her search for a real family, for the truth—to faith as the very dirt in which her father was buried alive.

Inez continues to explore the power of naming, the power of language to make and to alter worlds, by examining the traditions of other cultures. For example, in "The Woman Who Loved Worms," taken from a Japanese legend, the protagonist refuses the dictates of her tradition—"Disdaining butterflies/as frivolous,/she puttered with caterpillars" (18)—and realizes that her own handwriting—"Even the stationery/on which she scrawled/unkempt calligraphy" (18)—has the power to startle "the jade-inlaid indolent ladies" (18). By the end of her life her words have become indistinguishable from the processes of nature:

> Midge, tick and maggot words
> crowded her haikus
> and lines on her skin turned her old,
> thin as a spinster cricket. (19)

In a later poem, an "Old Woman, Eskimo," not only has the power to direct natural processes through her singing and sewing, she also realizes the effects on the landscape when she chooses to suspend these activities:

> Her singing makes
> the rain fall.
> Her sewing brings clouds.
> When she stops sewing,
> the green weather comes.
> When she stops singing,
> the white weather comes
> full of smooth threads
> to sew up her song. (35)

However, it is in the arena of language, specifically, of naming, that her most fundamental ability—to see—is rooted:

> She has seen birth,
> children waiting
> for their names.
> When she stops seeing,
> the snow needles come
> sewing the land
> to the hem of the sky. . . .
> The hides come undone
> all her songs are gone
> inside the rain
> for her children
> to hear later on. (35)

The separation of the brief tercet from the longer stanzas before and after it places particular autobiographical emphasis on Inez, as a child, waiting to be acknowledged or at least adopted, "waiting for [her] name" (35). This, in turn, becomes subsumed into the Eskimo folktale as the turn at which the old woman loses control over the landscape, when nature begins to progress without dictation, leaving the woman helpless, without sight and having lost her songs to the rain.

In "Nicolette," a piece Inez directs to the child she didn't have, the power of language to make manifest is again acknowledged, but this time the power resides in Inez's own poetry, in the final stanza:

> Nicolette, we will meet
> in my poem and when the light
> calls your name
> you will rise like a fern
> to live all summer long,
> a green integer
> in a pure equation of song.

Here Inez evokes the abilities of seeing, naming, and singing that belong to the Eskimo woman in a previous poem, but this time, because the child has not actually been born, the naming process residing in the poem belongs to the natural world as the poem makes it. Nevertheless, while the Eskimo woman's song is lost to the rain, this poem holds the power of resurrection and immortality in its fusion of natural processes and music.

Inez's belief in the power of naming was integral in her continual attempts to control the space of her body, beginning with her early childhood in the orphanage. There, the children were allowed "No dolls . . ./no spinning tops, tin/what-have-yous, wind-ups, anything" because the "nuns thought we would/quarrel" (72). To compensate, she gave her:

> ... fingernails names
> and jobs: old thumb, Pierre, the cop,
> pinkie Francine, slim-hipped one-note pianist.
> In my palms I loved the roads
> that led me to my realms: Lantasah, high
> in the reaches of Ti, Whoa and Neigh,
> crofts for my shires, stallions and nags. (72)

Not only did this naming process grant Inez, for a time, control of her personal space, it also, of course, provided a powerful imaginative escape from the relentless grip of that authoritarian atmosphere. However, while "Without Toys at the Home" illustrates the power of language to name and create, it also speaks the truth about the very real fragility of words in the face of physical oppression: "More than once I've/been found out. My cheeks still smart from/being caught" (73).

Perhaps the most poignant images in Inez's work spring from her efforts, through language, to either know her parents or have them know her, believing that love begins in knowledge, as in "River House Inventions":

> Blistered hands raw on the oars,
> I row past her house, call out her name. . . .
> I wave to the woman on the dock. (109)

And if finding her mother in this imagined scenario doesn't work— "'Curious,' she might say to a visitor . . ./. . . 'I saw a girl/wave to me from a boat. She called out my name./It was no one I knew'" (110)—she can always destroy the scene to make room for another:

> But I can annihilate the boat, make the river
> disappear, plant the house on a plateau or a hill.
> I can have the woman on the dock look out
> through French windows at the river and sky,
> make her believe in the power of prayer. (109)

She can even go so far as to:

> . . . re-invent my parentage. Not father-priest,
> but father-baker, hair the color of daily bread.
> Not mother-archivist, but mother-sailor-with-a-crew
> steering a course for the Argentine. (109)

But, as we know from her autobiography, Inez, while she never meets her father (the man who had become a monsignor in the Roman Catholic Church), she did actually meet with her mother several times; and the second time, as detailed in the penultimate stanza, resonates with distance and sadness:

> This is true. A proper daughter in a proper suit, I knock

> at her door for the second time in thirty years.
> We nod, pump hands, say where we've been.
> I don't know who she is and will not know even after death
> strolls up from the river to take her in his arms. (110)

Colette Inez claims in an autobiographical essay, after detailing the neglect and physical abuse she endured at the hands of first a foster mother and then a foster step-mother, that her only true refuge was in words:

> Thankfully there were books, always books, and I strongly believed in the power of language to change my reality.... I conscientiously copied out new words: stertorous, lambent, ptotic. I memorized these and other unfamiliar words, and invented paragraphs for them to live and work in. (185)

This belief had its natural genesis in a childhood spent in a strict Roman Catholic liturgical setting, where the power of naming is taken to Neoplatonic extremes in the concept of the Logos, the creative Word that, through a Christian lens, becomes manifest in Jesus Christ. And knowing, as she was eventually to learn, that her own father was a priest in that church left little doubt of the primary nature of language to her very survival, as she explains best in "The Entry of James Ensor into My Memories of Brussels":

> And the child I was asks: What am I to learn in the subtle world? And I answer her, to draw consoling words out of the air. To arrange them like irises in a vase, to weave them into proof our lives like a sea teem with remembrances. To endure. Integral and personal. (101)

Works Cited

Inez, Colette. Contemporary Authors Autobiography Series, Vol. 10: 179–197.
—. *Getting Under Way: New and Selected Poems.* Brownsville: Story Line Press, 1993.

John Harvey

An Unfocused Star

I.
"The reader participates in the joy of creation ...
That is the sign of creation."
Gaston Bachelard

Joy: some few years ago I received the gift of hours spent, over too few months, with Colette Inez. We shared books, poems, tastes.

I recall most an evening ride down a dark Ohio road, adjacent at times to a national forest. I was driving, and though I had to follow headlight beams, reflective highway dividing lines, I could not resist a cloudless, star-salted night sky.

Colette immediately, as usual, extended my casual observation into rhapsody, began to note which constellations were especially bright, in season.

I seem to recall Orion, unfocused by the prudent half-attention of a driver, by, perhaps, headlights in a rearview mirror, by memory. I seem to *wish* it were Orion, gaseous birthplace of bright stars—for here began my personal interest in Colette's celestial imagery, so visible throughout her poetry it invites "study." Are there predictable patterns, correspondences?

There are wonderful precedents and interplays: take the mother and father of American poetry, Dickinson and Whitman. There's the well-limned motif in Dickinson of arcs, horizons, circumference, found also in images of bird flight ("stars like birds staggered overhead" Colette says in one poem), related, Hyatt Waggoner has argued, to ideas of spiritual boundary, and Emerson's essay "Circles."

Whitman famously defines himself as a Cosmos. I delighted in Colette's playful allusion to Whitmanic style in the ironically titled (and themed) "Word Circuits, Solitary," "Look for my atoms in a school of fish,/a distant snow, a nebula's veil in a diffuse dream//in the marriage of great galaxies." She plainly has no "anxiety of influence," but invokes and includes. It would be naive to believe that past is not present.

Bachelard has claimed that a good book should be immediately reread. I recently spoke with a friend, also appearing in this collection of essays, of rereading Colette, of the close reading only writing can accommodate, and we agreed that the return—much less than immediate—has provided us with increased worth.

Lewis Hyde has acknowledged this of gifts; unlike commodities, or used cars, gifts increase in value through use. Although she employs self-mockery in her response to Whitman—"Language, a stay/against death. And I? Will I die/with a wreath of speech hung in a chapel for the bereaved,/clichés of lament arranged in a spray, a corsage/of nimble phrases pinned to my shroud?"—Colette's use of celestial imagery coincides with a permanence related to circularity, to an understanding of how gifts are consumed. Hyde tells us that "When we see that we are actors in natural cycles, we understand that what nature gives us is influenced by what we give to nature. So the circle is a sign of an ecological insight as much as of gift exchange."

Stars are like birds, and, in "My Priest Father's Words," Colette writes "in the circle//of birds, your *Historia Scholastica*/will vanish like these clouds." The circularity assists her turn into poignant affirmation, "each//a life with its own shadow/on the earth as in your name/for me, uncalled for daughter,//as in my name for you,/father, Father." The upper case in the poem's last address insists on the religious symbolism so easily, but so vitally, a consequence of her birth parentage. And the last line in the last poem in *Clemency*, "Transformations," reasserts natural cycle. What will happen when humans disappear from earth? "We will hide in a damp cocoon and start again." As Octavio Paz has observed, "Poetry seeks not immortality but resurrection."

II.

"The poetic act has no past." Gaston Bachelard

We *learn* to focus stars "historically" these days, a consequence of technology: their light arrives across eons, sometimes from a source diminished, or darkened entirely. Yet for many of us the immensity of a clear night sky, its celestial vertigo, dissolves in ambient light. There are advisory boards and journalistic postings on the issue of light pollution. The American Astronomical Society has a related committee; it proclaims that "the night sky is the heritage of all humanity, which should therefore be preserved untouched." To what extent *might* we touch a star? This is plainly not an empirical question, asks instead for a phenomenological description.

Colette Inez, a small girl living in a Brussels orphanage on the *Rue Chant D'Oiseau*, admires for the first time, astonished, the flock of stars soaring overhead; she does not even know the word "star," but hears the song in which it participates. Her response is profoundly primitive, unmediated. Later, she will learn doubt. As she has reported in "Monday's Children," she will come to think "the world flat, an orphanage floor." But initially, and more accurately, she feels wonder: the stars sing now (an inchoate recognition of the eternal, which has no past or future). She feels tragedy: she overhears their song (a nascent comprehension of her disasterous relation to eternity). She begins to sing: the stars are now part of her, a Cosmos. As Bachelard observes, "Grandeur progresses in this world in proportion to the deepening of intimacy."

Colette, writing of visiting her mother, ends her poem "Meeting in Nérac" with these lines:

> Ruler of wanderers and lanterns at night, let her study
> the comet one more time. I ask this for a woman of Nerac
> from whom I inherit a love of quandaries: my doubt
> of heaven, hers of the here and now. What else we meant
> to call into question or deny, stays unresolved
> like an unfocused star.

She, Colette—for autobiography provides her work with authority, a resonant power unavailable to many writing in the confessional mode, a psychic weight that is the ironic *donnee* of her family life as was that of Robert Lowell, a congruence of personal and larger impersonal forces—makes a request of some odd minor deity, who assists both those who travel and those who keep homelights burning. But why make a supernatural request if she doubts heaven? Specifically, she asks for her mother to study Halley's Comet one more time; since this second witnessing of the comet would put her mother at least in her mid-seventies, Colette is wishing her mother longevity.

Since, in turn, she visits her mother "after a long absence of years," it's fair to associate Colette herself with the comet: she wishes herself to become an object of study for her scholarly mother. Scholasticism: "a love of quandaries." Line break and syntax layer the meanings; Colette cherishes her spiritual doubt, *and* the mystery she confronts in her mother's doubt of things worldly, even the importance of her own daughter.

Despite a shared intellectualism, and so the potential for understanding, there's a spiritual dimension to Colette's secular anguish that perhaps her mother might learn from, for how can one experience a "dark night of the soul," and spiritual rebirth, if one does not *painfully* renounce the world, is emotionally indifferent to it? Colette quotes her mother and describes her mother's tone: "'The region is filled/with interesting ruins.' Her English accent rings/in counterpoint with the sigh of palms."

The final image of the poem is a technical counterpoint to its assertion; we experience poetic closure and the uncertainties of personal identity and relation simultaneously. The precision of a blurred image: her star gazing has been altered through intellectual apprehension and technology (for surely the star is unfocused not through some undefined inclemency of weather, but through a poorly adjusted telescope lens, maybe the Celestron 8 she mentions in another poem). Image becomes symbol, yet allegory (an orphan has first only the *idea* of a mother, a father) becomes realism.

Out of biographical necessity, out of self-affirmation in the context of her birth parents' forbidden coupling, Colette is (in "How Did They Recognize Autumn in the Dark of the City," a title which inverts notions of light pollution, yet confirms the consequences) "one who would celebrate the union of heaven and earth"; one who, indeed, would celebrate an act with no past.

Ill.
"Images of full roundness help us to collect ourselves ...
For when it is experienced from the inside, devoid of all
exterior features, being cannot be otherwise than round."
Gaston Bachelard

Patterns, meaningful motifs: the body of Colette's poetry establishes these so convincingly that it's reasonable to assert she achieves unity, roundness. The relative absence of celestial imagery in poems treating her adoptive parents in the United States (among many stylistic contrasts from other poems) only underscores her praxis.

It is her birth parents who, by virtue of his Catholic ordination as priest and her position as scholastic acolyte, their fall from vows, their distance from their daughter (Simone Weil proposed that "distance is the soul of beauty") merit the lovely and complex stellar symbolism. Colette directly identifies each of her birth parents with a star, her mother in "My Mother and Cartography," her fallen father a flower, a "Woodland Star," in "My Father in the West."

In a poem about life with her adoptive parents, celestial reference, in a fine pun on radio astronomy, occurs not in connection to those around her, but in longing for a truer relation to those who are not: "Huddled in that kitchen/with its empty fridge, I stare/at the back end of the radio, and tubes glow/like a miniature city of pure glass towers/sending messages of years out to the stars."

Colette announces her circumstantial connections to the heavens, stars, across constellations of poems. "No need to say I was resolved to be born/in a hot dance of summer,/tarantellas and polkas under spiraling arms/of the Milky Way," she reports of her second visit to her birth mother. No need, as her mother's reluctance to speak in personal terms allows but imagined resolutions.

Imagination, intellection: of the father Colette has not known, she regrets that "I cannot be there with my star charts to show him/the fleur-de-lis figure of Perseus, or Andromeda's blur," again the earthly lack of focus and connection, the eerie limits of technology, yet beautiful, "like milkweed dust."

And in a prose poem that bears resemblance to Native American prayers, more happenstance, "I will find the fish of miracles if someone tells how I came to be born in red moonlight, the eider duck's breast pressed to her eggs under the sign of the crab."

At her most skeptical she asserts, "Freak tricks, the stars, the moon."

At her most generous (perhaps in the company of, as I like to imagine but have little textual support for, her husband Saul) she will reply to her own direct query, in "Probings Under Vega," "the sky transformed to metaphor/makes us ask what is real?" with "God as an infinite machine seems possible/as we look straight up at blue-white Vega, one-fourth the age/of the sun, twenty-six light years away,/brightest summer star."

Kathleen Reilly

The Mirror and the Map: Colette Inez and the Orphan's Poetic Search

When I met Colette Inez in the fall of 1990 at Ohio University, I approached her after her reading, clutching my copy of *Family Life,* and confided to her that I had done it too: searched for and found the birthmother who had given me away. Inez must hear it frequently; no other poet, to my knowledge, has claimed this poetic territory. Betty Jean Lifton divides us into Good Adoptee/Bad Adoptee (57). I recognized in Inez a fellow Bad Adoptee and I was thrilled. We had refused to take "no" for an answer; we had defied society's taboos; we had peered beyond the veil of secrecy into our origins; we were Pandoras who had ignored the warning, "Do not open this box." In the language of the illegitimate, we had been lost, we had searched, we had found. She was kind enough to sign my book, "To Kathleen, who understands the search—in poetry." (But what do I understand? What did we find?)

How do other people read her, people with mothers, with fathers, who take for granted the family resemblance in the mirror? Our referents for "family," "father," "mother" aren't the same. Lifton writes of a conversation with a (nonadopted) friend: "She keeps seeing me as someone like herself and her other friends. I forgive her. That is the mistake all nonadopted people make" (4).

So I must admit at the outset nothing like objectivity. My perspective, reading, is skewed. Despite a Ph.D. and published poems, this essay is written by an abandoned child. I hold up Lifton as evidence: inside us lives a tiny official "orphan" who won't go away, the one who was "given away." Is she a gift? Does anyone want her? "Who will love you?" Inez writes (C, 18). The paradox is that I can read Inez's poems only as autobiography.

While it is tempting to set autobiography beside autobiography, history beside personal history, that will not ultimately be what matters. Already the phrase "orphan asylum," the place of my birth, rings like a social anachronism, vaguely Dickensian. Three of my students recently wrote personal essays about their proud assumption of the status of single motherhood; one wrote openly about her decision to abort. Another young man saw in his promiscuous father's legacy of successive wives and half-brothers of various races, religions, cultures, and lifestyles, a type of human brotherhood. Do bastards even exist anymore?

As a society, we are fascinated by reunions. I see son meet father on *Oprah;* tears tremble in a grown man's eyelashes. Women's magazines at the grocery checkout feature happy reunions, smiling faces, and tips to reunion registries online. We like to believe that family matters.

Such inheritance is double-edged. To be born in this context—illegitimate, given up—is to enter the world already embarked on the first stage of Joseph Campbell's monomythic quest of the hero with a thousand faces, separation. But are you a foundling or a changeling, Abraham deserted in the cave, Moses adrift in the bullrushes, or Oedipus, the Bad Seed? Are you Oliver Twist, lost and undergoing episodes of trials, to be ultimately recognized and enfolded in the ample bosom of family? In folk tales, are you "The Ugly Duckling" or, my personal childhood favorite, "The Goose Girl," carrying your handkerchief with the magical three drops of your mother's blood? The pattern is supposed to be separation, initiation, recognition, and return (Campbell, 329). We absorb it with our Grimm's fairy tales.

During the Journey, the child must face a long period of obscurity, danger and disgrace. Part of the trial engages the years of orphanhood, abusive fostering, and the frustration of the search itself. Poet-apprentice, the young Inez hero must also name the unnameable. Like the outcome of the Search itself, which simultaneously grants and withholds recognition, this poetic quest can only partially succeed.

In Inez's poetry of myth, the parents who are found are not so much the specific, "real," genetic parents, although they are, but progenitor and "Genetrix" (C, 41), the King and Queen, the parents within the self: animus, anima, the double, the shadow—a Jungian vocabulary becomes unavoidable. Parents are a mirror and a map, two images which Inez uses frequently, but a whole self is reflected, and recovered in the "mother country" (C, 49). Lifton writes, "All adoptees unconsciously search for that missing part of themselves, call it mother, father or twin" (41). The true quest is for individuation, the recognition of the I AM.

Why this is particularly crucial to us bastards, patriarchically defined, is because society and language itself have conspired to erase us. Significantly, Inez names herself "bastard" twice, once for each parent (FL, 6, 20). This is "the beast of the invisible" that troubles the "zero face in the mirror" (C, 90). We are silence, secret, the skeletal ghost in society's family closet. We are "orphans." We are, once parental rights are signed away, by law *as if dead* (Lifton, 16). We are renamed, unnamed. What's in a name? A life, as it turns out, a chimera of identity.

I remember holding for the first time, my adoption decree, which I had, in the course of my search, never been able to obtain. Here is my original name, Ellen, which I knew, and the name of my mother, which I found anyway. My life, the person I have become, began with this piece of paper. Here is the signature that changed Ellen to Kathleen. "After the earthquake," Inez writes, "they are given new names" (FL, 12). This is the evidence. Who is Kathleen? She is a word on a piece of paper.

Who is Reilly? She is the surname of a divorced husband ten years gone. Who is Kathleen Reilly? Does she even exist? She is a convenient fiction.

Where, then, is Ellen? Did she cease to exist? As I hold the paper, I feel her within me like a vestigial twin, a self-that-might-have-been. Inez, too, recognizes the other self, the other who is a third person. "In a province/of lost origins ... /the child I tap on the shoulder/turns to me with my own face" (FL, 11).

The camera's flash captures Ellen at the moment, decree not yet signed, new adopting mother smiling. In the faded gray photograph, Ellen looks bewildered. I know her eyes are blue. My eyes are blue.

I remember adopting my sister in the judge's chambers. Like Inez, we are "signed away" (FL, 4). "When I was born, my mother/hid me in a paragraph" (FL, 7). We learn quite early it is all done with language, a signature, a pen, a sleight of hand. This is how "The cuckoo abandons her eggs in an unfamiliar nest./I guard my secret names" (C, 79). This is when the separate burden of "The Chosen Baby" begins. One should, of course, be grateful to be spared the fate of orphanhood. But what is chosen can be unchosen. "'Too late to send her back with the war/going on ... The child's a mistake'" (FL, 27).

This is poetry written from "my bed of parentheses/in my house of lost rhymes" (FL, 7). To be "rich in words" is to break the silence of one's origins, to emerge from those parentheses as something incidental, accidental, hidden, not. Inez writes of her mother correcting her letters, her words "a message that refused/to be lost. Lost and found/... I used words, therefore I was, wasn't I?" (C, 43). I will note the question mark, impetus of the search. In the course of it one learns: words are knowledge. Knowledge is power. I am a word.

Two books, *Family Life* and *Clemency*, contain the poetry of this myth most completely. Ten years apart, both in three parts, they seem designed to mirror each other. The second is an obverse of the first, a reversed image, or like the negative of a photograph. What was bright becomes dark, a shadow reunion. *Family Life* gives us what Lifton calls "Adoptee as Survivor" (42), as Inez writes of herself "rescued from the past" (FL, 47). This is the version we want, but it is not true, or only partially true. It is the myth we first construct when we find, trying to integrate our origins into the person who exists in the external world. But poetry is of the internal world.

We bastards are quite adept at revising identities; we managed to be born in the first place as "orphans," without mother or father at all. The very term "the Search" is a code. In practice, it can mean writing letters, researching, trying to find the lost name, the last address, lying, being lied to, finally, in its successful phase, staring at a "blood stranger" who is your mother (FL, 3).

Physical resemblances, taken for granted by the rest of the world, fascinate us, and we're very good at seeing them. Resemblance is the "lost rhyme," an echo of shape, a likeness of face as of sound.

Resemblance *is* recognition, a mirror and a map. Here a mirror is not narcissism, but self-knowledge. I will never forget those first photographs of my birthmother—did my hand tremble as I slid them out of the envelope? For the orphan, "No mirrors allowed" (FL, 17). The fosterling sees the new family as "people not wanting her reflection in their mirror" (FL, 27). Inez keeps returning to likeness, as I do, seeing it even in the minutae, "a face that resembles mine/in one corner above the right eye/and in a temple vein" (FL, 3). She asks, with some anxiety, "Do I resemble you… A forehead's/width, do we share that" (C, 49).

But the resemblance is problematic. "A moment's glance reveals/I don't resemble her family branch" (C, 42). Inez mirrors her father. "Soon it was clear I favored him" (C, 63). This affects her acceptance:

> When I smile, does she recall
> my father's lips skimming her throat,
> narrow shoulders and breasts, full as mine
> under my sweater? Our talk is thin.
>
> How easy to slip into her design
> for making me invisible.   (C, 55)

I remember an early letter in which my birthmother expressed relief that I resembled her and her family so much. (Would they have accepted me if I had resembled my father?) With my hair cut short, I am almost the double of my grandfather and his first cousin, the Cardinal. My grandmother confides to me that she was adopted earlier in the century from the same home. Is there a gene for loving unwisely? Spookiest are the eyes—I meet a stranger with my eyes. "Nothing derelict in what the blood knows//repeating its feat of memory" (C, 90). I am not interested in how I resemble them, but how they resemble me. Touching my grandmother's arm in farewell is like touching my own skin. (Is this what it means, 'flesh of my flesh'?)

What does the orphan want? "I didn't want to die/I wanted to be recognized," Inez writes (FL, 47). "Reunion," the tenuous thread of letters from the birthmother, and the words at their meeting simultaneously grant and withhold that recognition.

> I look for a sign
> she has looked for me—
> letters returned
> addressee unknown.

> A photograph....
> "You may write to me,
> not saying who we are."   (C, 39)

The mother, too, a woman of her time and place, faces the awkwardness. "An old woman, she sits by the river in autumn/to write to a daughter she barely knows" (FL, 55). Inez acknowledges, "This isn't the journey I want" (C, 54). But the searcher cannot refuse the journey that is offered any more than, as Ted Hughes says, the poet can refuse the myth. Reunion, like orphanhood, occurs on *their* terms and is negotiated. The orphan, returning to break the silence, becomes a participant in complicity as another fiction is upheld. "You who now present me to your tenants as a friend/from America" (C, 50).

My birthmother, early on, told me she wanted me to call her not "mother" but by her name, as if we are merely adult friends of some acquaintance; she calls me by my adoptive name, never by the name she originally gave me, never "daughter." "My name, you never said to me.//You would not say who I was. /I told my story again and again, trying to get it clear" (C, 51).

Inez, too, is aware of treading into living memory, someone else's past. "There are questions I will never ask./There are answers she will never give" (FL, 3). Will silence and secrecy win after all? Is our very existence a reproach, something the mother doesn't want to remember? "'I'd almost forgotten,' she will sigh" (FL, 3). I was told, "We never spoke of it again." More than the orphan's birth is remembered.

But to imagine is to summon the ghost of the father. For Inez, as the photograph shows, the search for the father is imperative and major. Dead, he cannot truly be found, but only mythologized. Significantly, she places him not in a traditional Roman Catholic version of Purgatory to which his broken vow of chastity might entitle him a place (Purgatory, it is clear, is for the living), but in an older mythic land of the dead beyond the sea in the west. "I kneel,/astounded never to have gathered flowers for him,/nor blessed the seed, the mutiny of his fleshy root" (C, 65). Dead, his silence is absolute; he can never grant recognition; she is denied a daughter's place.

Knowledge "of" does not complete the quest. "What am I to make/of these facts of you, you who will never trace/my eyebrows or my mouth" (C, 66). She wants the word. "You never called me/daughter. I never called you father." Because their reunion cannot exist in the external world, it must occur in "the moment I invent: You snap off /your collar and turn, an ordinary father,/to embrace me in the garden" (C, 66). Yet I covet "these facts." To my initial questions, my grandmother, as spokesperson, wrote back that she and my birthmother had discussed the matter and decided that it would be better for me if I did not know. Secrets within secrets, a closed door. "What she won't say floods the room with images" (FL, 4).

The mother, too, withholds complete recognition, even after her death.

> After she slides into earth, nothing
>
> of his name, nor mine, not a scrap
> will be found in locked boxes or her vaults.
> None will guess a child had slipped out
> of those delicate thighs. And I will have my say. (C, 13)

Against such erasure, utterance is nothing less than a spell to hold the self in place.

Like the reunion with the father, the complete reunion with the mother must be fulfilled in words. The past must not be merely survived (though that is hard enough), but rewritten. "The past doesn't fit me," Inez concludes (C, 64). Another past is created, within the self. "In a dream of an arbor I must pass through,//she grants me supple words, she coaxes,/my daughter, she says, my lost child" (C, 63). The very word "reunion" is inaccurate, for the initial "union" was *in utero* and preceeds words. "Once I was your other heart, a double/tapping in your body when you tuned to the music/of my birth and we spoke without words" (C, 48). That is the truest communion, when poetry approaches the wordless, the moment of complete oneness when words become unnecessary.

Significantly, *Clemency* ends—or does it begin—with the imagery of gestation as well as revision (the processes are the same). In "Transformations," "ghost butterflies" are captured by the "lepidopterist": "He has seen our sort/before. Knobs, bumps, hairs, horns,/weren't we caterpillars once?" So far, the imagery is the familiar caterpillar transformed into a butterfly, and we are not surprised; butterflies are a traditional symbol for the soul, the psyche. Then we realize the imagery is unwinding backwards, from butterfly to caterpillar to grub. Suddenly a phoenix appears. The universe, too, participates in this transformation, sharing the butterfly word "flutter." We remember the orphan at the moment of the poem's act of reunion, reunited with the mother before birth in the communion of the wordless. "What then?/We will hide in a damp cocoon and start again" (C, 92). There can be no other answer to the question.

Works Cited

Campbell, Joseph. *The Hero with a Thousand Faces.* Cleveland, OH: World Publishing Company, 1956.

Emerson, Ralph Waldo. "The Poet." *Selected Writings.* NY: New American Library, 1965.

Hughes, Ted. "The Poetic Self: A Centenary Tribute to T.S. Eliot." *Winter Pollen.* NY: Picador USA, 1995.

Inez, Colette. *Clemency.* Pittsburgh: Carnegie Mellon, 1998.

—. *Family Life.* Santa Cruz, CA: Story Line Press, 1988.

Jung, Carl Gustav. *The Portable Jung.* ed. Joseph Campbell. NY: Penguin, 1971.

Lifton, Betty Jean. *Lost and Found.* NY: Bantam Press, 1981.

E. Barnsley Brown

"And I will have my say": Mother Loss and Mother Tongues in Colette Inez's *Clemency*

Nowhere is Colette Inez's work more powerful than in her search for the mother she did not know, the mother she endlessly creates and recreates, poetically fashioning identities for her like a child trying on new clothes. *Clemency*, in particular, devotes much more attention to Inez's mother than her father, a "husky man/in a clerical collar" (14) who appears in her poems, defined by the collar that shackles him to "the Order" (14) and whose allegorical import is not to be missed. Juxtaposed with this sterile, ratiocinative scholar is Inez's mother, parading in a multitude of roles with the facility of an experienced actress in a repertory company. The poet stages her mother's sexual encounter with her father as well as Inez's own encounter with her mother in later years as a means of claiming and disclaiming the woman who gave her up at birth, the woman who refused the role of mother. Inez effectively slips in and out of the womb, recreating the disparate moments of conception and rupture of the symbiotic bond between mother and child that led to her existence as woman, as scholar, as poet. Inez thinks back through her mother, searching for, even yearning for, language that will restore the bond that was severed long ago.

This search for such a language of restoration is beautifully rendered in the second poem of the collection, "A Story," in which Inez lyrically imagines her parents' meeting: the "priest old enough/to be her father" and "the Latinist/he needed for his work on medieval texts" (12). With the honesty of a writer who knows this is fictional story rather than fact, Inez envisions,

>When her clothes strained at the seams,
>both may have talked of crossing
>the border into Belgium.
>I don't know. No one must know,
>
>they agreed, except their confessor,
>and a colleague or two. (12)

The secrecy of this pair of surreptitious lovers who plan to rid themselves of the "evidence" of their union is juxtaposed with Inez's defiance, a defiance that rescues this poem from sentimentality: "I grew where flowers took root in dry fields" (12). Turning the barren ground of her own abandonment into fertile poetic soil, Inez continues,

> Soon the priest will be buried near the sea.
> but my mother would grow old, recording parchments
> and tomes on the history of the church.
> After she slides into earth, nothing
>
> of his name, nor mine, not a scrap
> will be found in locked boxes or her vaults.
> None will guess a child had slipped out
> of those delicate thighs. And I will have my say. (13)

Here, Inez strips her father of any paternity other than that bestowed by the church, calling him generically "the priest," while her mother is reduced to little more than a transcriber, growing old like Bartleby the Scrivener until "she slides into earth" into "nothing," a beautiful sleight of hand achieved by Inez's masterful use of enjambment from one quatrain to the next. Although no record of their sexual liaison and Inez's birth will be left by her mother, Inez, as poet, will set the record straight, a point underscored by the monosyllabic force of the final decree: "And I will have my say."

This story, the story of Inez's parents and her creation, while not under her control before—"Nothing I do will change them" (14)—becomes the poetic province of the writer who alternately hungers for and spurns the parents, particularly the mother, who would give up a child. Raised in a Catholic orphanage before being sent to live with a foster family in the United States at the age of eight, Inez characterizes her poetic process as "A kind of repeated exploration of the void: the parents that weren't, the rearing that had no foothold on bloodlines or genes" (Gorman 210, 217–18). Inez's emotionally charged subject matter results in poems that are oddly redemptive and accusatory, a kind of double-voicing of both compassion and betrayal. Inez explains, "I sometimes think of autobiographical poetry as 'tamed dreams.' The nightmarish vision of a slaughtered parent, the mayhem that the nighttime unconscious looses, is defused in the poem to make the message more sane, literate, less savage. To be honest, I still tap a reservoir of both pity and rage—toward both parents" (Gorman 219).

This reservoir becomes evident, once again, in "Last Trolley Stop, Brussels," as Inez dramatizes her physical and psychological migration to America. The abruptness of the move is emphasized in the clipped tercet that comes, like a musical bridge, near the middle of the poem: "The war arrives, breaks us apart./Three blasts of a ship's horn/and I salute another continent" (22). Yet the residual psychological effects of this forced migration are manifested in the elegiac tone of the rest of the poem, as Inez laments the loss of her mother tongue: "Not to open those soft books/in my first tongue" (22). Inez associates this loss with the loss of her parents, especially her mother:

> Never to find my father
> leaning against the rail
> of a ship, his arm slung
> about my shoulder, not
> to think our kisses wake my mother
> from her trance. Not
>
> to have pressed her limp hands
> to my face. (22)

The curious impotency of Inez's mother, whose "limp hands" dangle at the end of a line and whose trance renders her a mere ghost of a person, is contrasted with the clear details of the final section of the poem:

> Pages turn the stories I invent.
> I need to recall a tangerine red dress
> and sailor-blue coat, the sky over Brussels
> thrumming news of my trip. (23)

For Inez, writing is a comfort, a means of both inventing and remembering the past, recalling as well as calling it back to her in its palimpsistic forcefulness.

Inez concludes the poem with a migration back to the present, the past hidden beneath this topical reality:

> Now after a long fever, I turn
> towards my husband.
> We will catch the next boat, I say.
> On my childhood street furrows of grass
> camouflage the trolley tracks. (23)

In this stanza, Inez gives herself control over the next migration, a migration she will make with her husband. Yet this future migration is informed by her nostalgic movement back in time, assuring her of the presence of the past beneath the surface of the present, a point beautifully rendered in the poem's final metaphor: "furrows of grass/camouflage the trolley tracks." While before, "Pages turn the stories I invent," here Inez turns the poem back to the present, to the life over which she does have control as adult, woman, and poet.

In effect, "Last Trolley Stop, Brussels" beautifully sets up the second section of *Clemency* in which Inez encounters her birth mother years later, imagining and reimagining her in a series of well crafted poems. Of these, three in particular stand out for their vivid imagery, intertextual resonances, and narrative power. In "Oxford Meeting," "Writing Letters to My Mother," and "Hands," we are offered a keen awareness of "language as a survival mechanism" (Gorman 212), a means for Inez to cope with the deleterious effects of her abandonment. As a critic writes of one of Inez's earlier collections, *Family Life*, "Inez's obsessive return to her family story attests to her need to make sense out of the (ultimately intractable) narrative of her abandonment" (Fox 53). This abandonment haunts Inez, personified in the many faces of the mother she creates, over and over, in section two of *Clemency*, a mother who "communes/with a spirit/just past my gaze" (39), "A secret mother who'd waived the rights/to count the buttons of my coat" (41).

The first poem of section two, "Oxford Meeting," with its terse lines and taut images, presents the adult Inez meeting her mother for the first time in an Oxford lodging house, a setting which emphasizes the impersonal nature of this reunion. Inez writes,

> She asks what I want.
> I look for a sign
> she has looked for me—
> letters returned
> addressee unknown.
> A photograph. (39)

Instead of these mementos for which Inez scours the room, "The wall clock/hatches an hour" (139). Subtly, Inez uses the verb, "hatch," to imbue the clock with motherly tendencies while she describes her mother merely as "this woman," thus emphasizing their estrangement. Inez describes,

> Streaked white mane,
> disheveled at the neck,
> this woman
>
> was the furtive girl
> fingering her rosary,
> buttons strained
> when she took
> the train north
> to place me in a cradle
> strangers might rock. (39)

Aside from asking Inez what she wants, the only dialogue that this very distant specter of a mother speaks in the poem is "'You may write to me,/not saying who we are'" (39–40). Inez's love and hate for her biological mother are embodied in the final lines:

> She sees me to the door.
> Pallid roses of snow
> fall as I leave.
> I hunger for the color
> of fire, orange balloons
> floating through ashes. (40)

The oxymoron of "roses of snow" and the image of the child's "orange balloons/ floating through ashes" bring home Inez's yearning, her "hunger" for a redemptive relationship with her mother, one that would let her forgive and overcome her childhood abandonment.

Inez attempts to construct this redemptive relationship through language, as is evident in "Writing Letters to My Mother" in which Inez struggles to encompass her mother's state of mind and experience:

> What words must I pluck from a box of nouns
> to suggest my mother's weltanschauung when she packed
> me off to the nuns? Pain. Anger. Regret.
> What are their referents? (58)

Searching for words to make palatable the unpalatable—namely, how her mother could choose to give to her up—Inez characterizes her poetic process as "Verbal *cul de sacs.*/I've dug them with my words to her" (59). Her words are signifiers, endlessly circling, never reaching a final, comfortable Signified: "Sometimes, my pen hovered over the page/like a dragonfly looking for a place/to land" (59). In effect, Inez's world is "This blue marsh of language" (59), a desolate landscape that she must make fit for her own birth, her own conception and development as woman, poet, and scholar.

In "Hands," Inez moves from including her mother as a shadowy character in her poems to directly addressing her: "You, who once took my hand lightly in yours/but let it slip away" (60). While before, her mother has haunted her poems, here she is the recipient of Inez's letter, Inez's poem in which she does, at last, have her say. Although the imagined mother throws Inez's symbolic letter in the river, Inez details what she would do, had she the opportunity:

> Yet, old woman who never said my name,
> I say if I could drop down beside you,
>
> I would cover your hands in mine.
> I would pull out the combs
> to let your hair fall like a cloak,
>
> all in a rush. (60)

Inez here achieves, poetically, what she desires, dropping down beside her mother through tightly constructed tercets that simultaneously express as well as contain her rage. Language becomes the means of approximating a reunion with her mother, however riddled with pain that meeting may be. Inez explains, "Full of longing, my phrases, like my hands,/keep their distance from your fear" (60). Hers is a language of yearning, a language that strives to uncover the mother that was lost before, if only as an image that flickers between and among poems.

Works Cited

Fox, Suzanne. "A Child Singled Out for Departure." *Parnassus: Poetry in Review* 15.2(1989): 52–65.

Gorman, Jim. "An Interview with Colette Inez." *Parnassus: Poetry in Review* 7.1(1978): 210–23.

Inez. Colette. *Clemency*. Pittsburgh: Carnegie Mellon UP, 1998.

——. *Family Life*. Santa Cruz: Story Line Press, 1988.

Susan Sindall

Clemency: Poems by Colette Inez

American Book Review, Vol. 20, No. 4, May/June 1999

Scrutiny of one's family, parents in particular, is an obsession in current American poetry; as the roles we inherited rumble below our feet like tectonic plates, we sift the past for clues. Long-hidden neglects or childhood abuses may erupt.

In this luminous collection, Colette Inez looks closely at her origins with an impassioned curiosity. She's never simply accusative; poems are without self pity. Instead, she says, with an earned, calm simplicity: "I have found a way to tell the story."

The book, as well as individual poems, moves through life cycles. In the final poem, "Transformations," humans become Monarchs under the eye of a godlike lepidopterist and return to cocoons. The opening poem, "Refrain for My Sires," envisions her parents as lovers and leaps to her own "closed eyes, tongue numb, their flesh in the grass."

This bridge, from their unthinking act of conception to her own death, is an example of the many bridges she builds between disparities; some are common to us all, such as different life stages. She has a special sense for inherent divisions and a drive to unite them, as these lines from "The Telling" suggest:

> Inside her body, a fury of division seizes
> attributes from each: yellow-brown eyes,
> a fringe of auburn curls
> bloom into the parcel delivered to the Sisters.

"The parcel" we know as Colette Inez lived at an orphanage in Belgium. In *Getting Under Way*, she describes the nuns as "cunning and alert," serving "phlegmy" eggs to the children, once a week. Although the language has the humor of perfectly precise description, "Belgian Flicks" is more poetic anecdote, as are the three poems about the orphanage that precede the wonderful "Last Trolley Stop, Brussels."

Strands of history woven together this seamlessly should not have the pattern broken by excerpting single threads. As the poet recalls the orphanage, she also sets memory free with her dreaming, elegiac tone, "Not to slide into the morning/half awake, shaken by bells in the tower."

When World War II arrives, she's sent to America and loses "those soft books" in her first language. No sooner spoken than released.

The narrative turns, but her tone dreams on; having been forced to let her early childhood go, she's ready to release the parents she's never known but longed for, "Never to find my father/leaning against the rail."

Their kisses will never "wake my mother." This poem's level-eyed look into inevitabilities that are not death, but as harsh—the death of one's dearest dreams—is typical of this poet at her finest. She concludes with an image reminiscent of Carl Sandburg's "Grass," working hard, and unsuccessfully, to cover the dead of multiple wars: "Pile the bodies high at Austerlitz and Waterloo." In the Brussels she is visiting years later, the grass has done what it can: "On my childhood street furrows of grass camouflage the trolley tracks."

Inez has written vividly about her parents in many earlier poems. In the four sections of "Event Horizons" in *Family Life*, she tenderly imagines their arrivals. Her infant father "is one/with his desires." Her mother "needs no coaxing to arrive/in the afternoon's aroma of lavender and mint." This is a sorrowful irony; her father was a priest who seduced her naive mother, and they never married. Here, she is able to visualize their births, and her own, as unique moments. But the nuns teach the little "orphan" to say, "mea culpa, I regret/not being pure under a snow of bloomers and bibs." She has begun to internalize some inborn, inevitable guilt. By the end of this quiet poem, she's set out to "escape the custody of the past"—which she fully accomplishes in *Clemency*.

She never met her father. His clerical collar appears often as an emblem of restraint, as in the earlier "A Collar Rounds My Thoughts" in *The Woman Who Loved Worms*. It's as if she herself was being cut, suffocated, by her contemptuous rage. This collar "rounds my world/like an equator/burning to know your life."

In five consecutive poems, *Clemency* seeks, questions, and re-imagines this father; these poems openly embrace the paradoxical, without any loss of precisely seen detail. In "Reveries While Landing on the Coast," the poet directs her sensuous experiences at Mass to find him: "I believed/god lived in my mouth, in its membranes." She imagines how he may have seen his parish "a mammouth wave gathering/from a rift, dragging crosses and candles/out to drown." Although not more than a biological "sire" to her, perhaps he had burdens as a pastoral father. In the last stanza she says, "The past doesn't fit me" and dreams "of a daughter putting aside regret." In "My Father in the West," she allows him the cleric's traditionally keen knowledge of medicinal plants and is "astounded never to have gathered flowers for him." As if thinking about him for the first time, her insights here are fresh, amazed by her discoveries. In "My Father in a Garden," he removes his collar. He turns towards her, "an ordinary father,/to embrace me in the garden." It's as if the starched collar's ends had finally grown into two, loving hands.

Poems to, and about, her mother are spread throughout the book. They did have an actual, if distanced, relationship; there are wonderful poems here about her mother's relatives ("A Place at the Table" and "Gascon Voices," are both favorites). Unlike the always-dead father, the mother ages; she enters as a young woman, blindly in love "kissing the welts/where his collar cut./Her moans are woven of fur and bone."

All the poems are sympathetic to both parents' sexual passions.

In "Oxford Meeting," the actual mother invites the poet upstairs in a rooming house. She wears "Rumpled hose, elbows/poking through holes/of a potato colored/cardigan." She seems to have cared little for her daughter, makes no eye contact now; they seem as unlike as any two women could be. The poet's vitality bursts through the end of the poem: "hunger for the color/of fire, orange balloons/floating through ashes." There's tremendous relief; this daughter seems to know how distinct she is from her mother.

No matter what their particular circumstances, every mother-daughter bond seems forced to incorporate mixed emotions. Questions of identity abound. At some point in any woman's life, she looks in the mirror and asks, "Who is *she?*"

In "Empress in the Mirror," *(The Woman Who Loved Worms)* an elegant, rather cruel muse-self is seen "Floating her pen on linen paper." She's trapped in the glass. The speaker kneels in front of her. They're frozen in a hierarchy of misery.

"Found Child" and "Mirror Story" face each other like reflections in *Clemency*. In the former, the speaker says, "I nod to the girl I was" and is in danger of fainting from too much prayer and fasting. She is kind, tolerant, maybe a little patronizing as an older person, smiling down at the over intense child. At the end, as she easily leaves this younger face on a pillow, "moonlight smooths like a doting mother,/even now she tugs at my sleeve." In the latter poem, she sees herself in the mirror as a bruised young woman: "A man's hand leaves marks on her." There's broken glass from previous fights. In the final stanzas, she finally leaves her mirror prison. Now she turns her back on this former self: "I have found a way to tell the story./She would not know who I am."

Absent mothers have to be invented, or found in substitute figures; many of these poems feature Inez's foster grandmother, staying on her feet with "two canes and a Midwestern will to stay." Nana's a character; her stubborn scowl and demanding voice are very present, bossing everyone around. But Dee, the foster mother, calls up special longing.

She's appeared in earlier books: a violent, colorful, undependable alcoholic. "Dee's Migraines" is rich with ambivalence and a strange fascination. Dee is abusive and bangs the child's head on the wall for using her cologne. But the lines "cherry wood/gleam of your thick pageboy" and "ice blue satin nightie's V/dives between U-shaped breasts" evoke the passionate crush a teenaged girl develops on the woman she feels she may want to become, and Dee's pain, her "ally."

In the third, final, and shortest section of the book, the poet looks in the mirror again. "Consolation of Blood and Irises" gathers many selves in a tender, painterly embrace. The flowers in a vase are "some arrangement of Inez." By following the true self in her blood, she has written and re-envisioned until discovering that "Few consolations/arrive without words." This is not a poem to paraphrase; among its many beauties is a profound self-recognition and a quiet acceptance of a life-long love affair with words.

Although some of the strongest poems in *Clemency* have nothing obviously to do with parents or the progress of the self, the scope of "In Praise of Outlines" and dreamlike, speculative "Things Dream of Their Likenesses and Needs" suggest that the poet is inhaling fresh air, going on with renewed perceptions.

In the former, she personifies America, Central and South America, Antarctica, Southeast Asia, and Australia—and pulls the camera back through her own kitchen window that looks out on the Milky Way "advancing/from north to south like two peninsulas,/like coral reefs."

Along the way, she steps into, imagines, and sails herself with grand ease across the animated map. In the latter, she gathers a progression of images that somersault inside each other in a meditation on the afterlife. Bees brush legs to become dust from a disappearing comet. The intersections of what we wonder about may not be visible, but they can be imagined: "Desire devours my days. I change positions/in a bed which dreams intersecting points/and nodes."

"Things Dream of Their Likenesses and Needs"—and this collection—is filled to the brim with Inez's pleasure in the sensuous world. Like gardens in mid-summer, bees, birds, flies and gnats nearly collide in the richly scented air. Her experience, and satisfaction, with the spit and zing of tasty language is a continual strength in her work. Her vitality stays high through every word: her curiosity persists. Her passion towards clear-sightedness drives the lines. In some wonderful paradox of maturity, she's ventured into familiar areas with fresh energy and depth.

Lili Corbus Bezner

The Image as Memory: The Use of Photography and Painting in Colette Inez's Poetry

Colette Inez's poetry evokes a visual world of art with subtlety and unselfconscious ease. Adjectives and metaphors referring to film, painting, drawing, and color are abundant, as shadowed tonalities and primary hues enrich memories of the past and ruminations of the present. And one long poem, "The Entry of James Ensor into My Memories of Brussels," succinctly ties her life with that of the Belgian painter. Photographs, in particular, provoke Inez to enter richly subjective territories of the mind, becoming the memento mori of her childhood. Exploration of Inez's symbolic use of family photography and Ensor uncovers her unique ability to transform the visual into the poetic.

Photography, since its invention in the 19th century, has become a well-worn but seldom analyzed motif in 20th-century poetry. For poets motivated to explore the self, the passage of time, and genealogy, family photography, in particular, offers an enriching territory of investigation given the accidental "slips of the tongue" often found as one gazes into the still faces contained in snapshots. Julia Hirsch has written extensively on the history and influence of family photography in this century. In *Family Photographs: Content, Meaning, and Effect* she discusses these seemingly banal photographs tucked away in almost all contemporary homes. Family photography, she writes, "celebrates the details, while it obscures the ironies, ambiguities, and contradictions of life" (45). While many viewers may discount such mundane images as mainstream or idealized, Hirsch confirms their complexity as signifiers of materialism, social values, and codified behaviors:

> [family photography] invites our curiosity about personalities and relationships but cannot fully satisfy it.... The picture, with its display of eyes and hands, perhaps even bosoms, groins, and legs, seems to bring intimacy without any formal introductions. But this is a superficial closeness. We have no more than a set of poses, of textures, to go on, and we recognize, finally, that the picture, like the faces we see on the television screen when the sound has been turned off, tell us only the

barest of narratives. And yet for all its limitations, it can be a narrative of great intensity. (6–9)

Hirsch's words link well with contemporary poetic explorations of photography and family. While family snapshots may inspire serious contemplation and allow entry into a barely-existent realm of relatives and relationships for many poets, ultimately they are conceptual fragments that cannot obscure ironies of life. While a professed objectivity stares one in the face (clearly described figures, material goods, the physical surroundings), another less articulated quality hovers below the photograph's surface—the inchoate interactions and relationships between those pictured. We may *see*, but can we *know* these figures?

A key source in contemporary criticism on the complexity and ambiguity of family photography is French philosopher and semiotician Roland Barthes. In *Camera Lucida* Barthes explores the metanymic and metaphoric sign systems inherent in photography. In true deconstructivist fashion, Barthes is uninterested in technique and aesthetics, the "blah-blah," as he calls it, of historians or sociologists. Instead, like Inez or other poets dealing with family photography, Barthes allows for and wallows in complete subjectivity in his interpretations; photographers' intentions are not discussed, nor the time period or social conditions inherent in the image. The "referent" and sole "mediator for all Photography," Barthes becomes the subjective center of all discourse into the medium: "As Spectator, I was interested in Photography only for 'sentimental' reasons; I wanted to explore it not as a question (a theme) but as a wound: I see, I feel, hence I notice, I observe, and I think" (21). And while scores of photographic writers have addressed the family snapshots of others (Michael Lesy's *Wisconsin Death Trip* comes to mind), Barthes contemplates images from his own family albums, as does Inez.

Family photographs, specifically, allow Inez to contemplate the cartography of her youth, a biography that consistently invades her poetry. Abandoned by her French mother, who was impregnated by a priest, she was raised in an orphanage only to "discover" her family and its profound secrets as an adult years later. Given her mother's inability to satisfy (much less nurture) Inez's desires for a more complete relationship or even acknowledge the potential of realizing a loving relationship, photography becomes the only symbolic means by which she can solidify a bond with a mother *manquée*.

Almost every one of Inez's poems dealing with photography concerns her own life; photography becomes a primary mimetic device to enter the world of her own abandonment by her parents and, most particularly, her mother. In her prose poem, "The House of Dreams," Inez writes, "My mother's house beckons me to the other side of the bridge crossing the Garonne./ Why am I hunting for photographs that don't exist?" She describes several imaginary photographs she longs for: loving images of her parents together (even as "two-backed beasts"), picking flowers, hugging their child Colette, growing old amidst roses in a light-filled world. Instead, however, the moon gestures, like an artist, "dab[bing] at the dark as if it were a wound. This isn't the journey I/want. The photographs sleep at the bottom of a box in my mother's house of dreams." In the end, there is no visual "proof" or record of a past together, no documentation of physical and emotional connection; only *longing* for the codified visions of family that such photographs can offer.

In "A Fairy Tale Country of Palaces," Inez constructs a fabrication of herself as a princess exiled because she reminds her mother too much of her birth father. As so often happens in her poems dealing with photographs of her parents, genetic links relating to biological features ("concupiscent lips, recalcitrant chin" "amber in my eyes, my temple vein," "her narrow shoulders") become her referents of belonging to these two strangers. Barthes, too, acknowledges photography's power in "proving" existence through biological ties. "The Photograph," he writes, "gives a little truth" including "a genetic feature, the fragment of oneself or of a relative" (103). For Inez, this function is profound. In "The Wig of Liliane," too, a cousin "proves" lineage through Inez's "mother's eyes," "the lift of the brow." In lieu of emotional ties, genetic likenesses, discovered through photographs, become significant links connecting dispersed lives. As Barthes puts it, photography "authenticates the existence of a certain being" (107); the photograph for Inez becomes the only vestige of these lives long past. But connections between these lives are tenuous and imaginary: "Photographed," she writes in "A Fairy Tale," "on her [mother's] veranda, I saw myself/fingering her manuscript," until, in dream only, she is coaxed into her mother's arms, the "lost child."

There is an extreme pathos in Inez's fantasies since they live only in her imagination, born of the fictive contents in a few old photographs. But in the realm of memory, visualized in the words of her poetry, mother, father, and child are joined, the poems themselves replacing the photographs never taken. The twist: after childlike reveries culminate, as in *Clemency,* Inez's "past grows cold./I clasp another woman's hand in mine/as if she were my child." While a visual world of photographs seems to comfort, to inspire, and to conjure loving bonds, ultimately such desires seem to falter as Inez faces the inadequacy of her own imagination to make the past change. Hirsch notes that "Family photographs themselves do not change, only the stories we tell about them do" (5). What changes is not the image in the photograph (real or imagined) that Inez views, but the perception of her reality.

"A Place at the Table" recounts seeing family photographs of cousin Maurice,

Aunt Jeanne and her sister, taken long before, one supposes, the family knew of her existence. Inez "superimposes" herself into this visual record of family, as a "seedling, posed with grandparents" and other loved ones. Again, Inez "enters" this imaginary "frame" filled with "imagined kisses" and familial intimacy. The love must be constructed, willed into being through imagination as it contemplates old photographs. In "After the Cantata Sounds Its Last Alleluia," Inez recounts seeing her "only picture of my father." She kisses the idolatrous image but knows "he won't ever come to feel/the thin skin of my kiss." Her mother, too, enters this field of memory, frozen in photographs Inez "frame[s] in a revery" of invented memories from the "lovechild ... she barely knows."

Barthes' analysis also centers on his viewing images of his own mother. Unlike Inez, however, Barthes enjoyed a long and deeply connected maternal relationship. However, upon seeing images of his (now dead) mother, he is stunned by their power to cloud rather than reveal any "reality." Key, also, to both Barthes and Inez, is the hovering metaphor of death in many family photographs. Barthes maintains that the "root" of photography is "return of the dead" as cameras are "clocks for seeing" (9, 15). As he contemplates his dead mother's face, alive in still photographs, he writes, "what I have lost is not a Figure (the Mother), but a being; and not a being, but a quality (a soul): not the indispensable, but the irreplaceable" (75). These words parallel Inez's conjured spirits of her mother in particular; we know as we read her work that she is not merely inventing a fantasy, but trying to "know" a living being that can never be known. The melancholy becomes as enormous for those reading her poems as it may be for Inez herself.

If "every photograph is a certificate of presence," then, as Barthes writes (87), Inez's photographically inspired poems authenticate lives that we (or she) can never know. Even when a viewer "knows" the subject in a photograph, as Barthes knew his own mother, our interpretations and understanding of their "reality" is compromised by our own subjectivity. As Barthes gazes at his mother's face, he is frustrated by not "finding" her:

> I recognized her differentially, not essentially. Photography thereby compelled me to perform a painful labor; straining toward the essence of her identity, I was struggling among images partially true, and therefore totally false. To say, confronted with a certain photograph, 'That's *almost* the way she was!' was more distressing than to say, confronted with another, 'That's not the way she was at all.' The *almost:* love's dreadful regime.... (66)

Inez, too, must struggle with the *almost,* the presence of absent figures, and so spins fairy tales out of small black and white moments staged before old cameras. The image, at least, confirms existence. The poem affirms life into the images. Like Barthes, Inez seeks truths, however small, in the photographic likenesses she draws for us. "If my efforts" to read photographs, Barthes said, "are painful, if I am anguished, it is because sometimes I get closer, I am burning: in a certain photograph I believe I perceive the lineaments of truth" (100). Barthes and Inez, kindred spirits, penetrate the visual codes framed before them in photographs. But neither is reckless enough to secure absolute meaning; instead each writes of possibility, ambiguity, contradiction.

Inez's allusions to photography are related, almost exclusively, to her biographical poems concerning her own family (or lack thereof). However, in "Daughter's Photo in an Old Folks Home" a photograph evokes the past in another familial context, as its frame becomes a passageway into others' lives, even those long dead. Inez, as usual, is not interested in the actuality of the figures, or what Barthes calls their *studium* (detached cultural or historical factness), but in their metaphoric possibility, their *punctum*. Punctum, according to Barthes "is that accident which pricks me (but also bruises me, is poignant to me)" (22). In presenting the photograph to her readers, Inez describes the image's punctum by layering symbolic strata onto an imagined landscape. The family photographs, ultimately, whether dealing with her own history or that of others, become knots of conflict and repression, hardly positivist vistas of happy allegiances. Inez understands all too well the photograph's power to create, or destroy, familial bonds; even as she weaves together image and tale, the visions unravel, complicated testaments to the profound chaos of life.

Barthes writes that "Photography is unclassifiable ... it aspires, perhaps, to become as crude, as certain, as noble as a sign, which would afford it access to the dignity of a language." But, he adds, "a photograph is always invisible: it is not it that we see" (6). His words resonate in context to Inez's poetry; we may share her discovery of these framed images, but we never *see* them or even truly know that they exist as described to us. Inez invests seemingly objective visions with life, creating tableaux vivant of memory.

Family photographs, then, are not merely subjective Rorschachs upon which Inez interprets positive banalities and happy idealized notions of family; they disturb and puncture their own professed sense of the ideal. In "Grandmother and Child Are Set to Listen on Sunday Nights," a photograph of the grandmother's son provokes reverie into his sexual abuse of the child, and the grandmother's own father's "hands under the coverlet." It would be far easier, in Inez's poems, for photographs to engender clichéd or ego-aggrandizing ideals; but given her childhood history, she seems to realize that "family" can be invented or dissected with the sharp instruments of her words.

Photography provides Inez a fertile and fictive window into the world of relationships, biographies, and memories that do not exist, or exist uncomfortably, and become born through the act of sight combined with creative thought. "Red August Letter" recounts a dream in which a friend is "a photographer/in a darkroom developing shots I couldn't/quite make out. I asked how you balanced/opposing needs." The contrasting polarity of black and white, the photograph's professed clarity blurred by indistinct forms again points to this medium's forceful presence in Inez's work as a visual stimulant and as a metaphor of creativity and ambiguity.

Inez, despite what some may see as an over-reliance on her life's history in her poetry, moves into a more universal realm of survival and spirit by confronting the *almost* Barthes laments. In "The Dreamforest" Inez again contemplates another photograph that provokes analysis of the sad childhood endured and seemingly made bearable by virtue of her strong imagination. While now, readers might say, Inez puts that imagination to creative use in her poetry, in her childhood it encouraged the creation of fictional family biographies, heroic tales, and familial connection that made existence bearable. The ability to transcend existence through imagination, one realizes, saved her. In "Belgian Flicks" Inez disparages the notion of orphaned children restricted from the pleasures of joy, creativity, and imagination, again within the context of a photographic metaphor: "I lived eight years or more/with the Catholic Sisters in Belgium/and never saw a movie" she recites, in defiance of their rules and uninspired lack of "possibilities."

Inez consistently utilizes the visual language of art, even beyond photographic metaphors; painterly and sculptural terms and images infuse her poetry, linking the creativity of art to personal memory. In one of her longest poems, also her most thorough analysis of a specific artwork, "The Entry of James Ensor into My Memories of Brussels," Inez combines quotations from the artist with her own reflections, conflating their troubled years in Belgium. The associations between the two create dynamic parallels reinforcing Inez's perceptions of being the lonely outsider, the rejected orphan.

Ensor (1860–1959) was a Belgian painter often associated with the Symbolist movement in *fin-de-siecle* Belgium. During these years in the 1880s, Baudelaire labeled imagination as "the queen of faculties" and helped promote the Symbolist movement of writers and artists for whom decadence and personal vision reigned (Lesko, 4). Rejected by the Belgian academy as well as the avant-garde as heretical and outrageous, Ensor epitomized the lonely modernist attempting to push artistic expression into new and higher symbolic realms. His disturbing and obsessive fantastical scenes of domestic bourgeois interiors, skeletons, persecution, torture, and spiritual poverty, conceived in acrid colors and expressionistic brushwork, created intensely personal canvases that shocked his peers.

When his most celebrated work, *The Entry of Christ into Brussels in 1889* (1888), was rejected by the avant-garde group of Belgian artists, Les Vingt, he withdrew from the art world. In provincial Ostend he lived above his mother's chinoiserie shop which was filled with knickknacks and Bergman-esque masks used to celebrate carnivals. Masks, a repeated icon in Ensor's work, became a popular Symbolist motif in the 1880s and 1890s. They animate his canvases, creating caricatures of moral ugliness and social indictments on human duplicity and hypocrisy (Lesko, 21; McGough, 55, 163). Not only were such images considered scandalous (the government threatened to close his shows)—critics were unappreciative; in *Dangerous Cooks* Ensor painted his own head on a platter to be served to a table of critics.

The Entry of Christ into Brussels in 1889 depicts the second coming of Christ in modern day Brussels. The huge canvas (8'5" x 12'5") is dense with figures; it depicts a world of congestion, confusion, and irrationality. Jesus is a mere speck of a man on a tiny mule, almost ignored by the throng of grotesque humanity and overwhelmed by human chaos. In this complex painting loaded with layers of personal meaning and assaulting all conventions of beauty, a disorderly and hostile modern society is "unmasked."

Why is Inez attracted to this artist and his painting? She ironically twists his original title in her own poem and includes significant quotations by Ensor before entering her own memories of her early years in Belgium. The first quotation by Ensor that she selects establishes her admiration for his contrary spirit: "My colors are purified ... integral and personal. Yet I upset convention ... I was called nasty, bad ... a simple cabbage became obscene; my placid interiors ... hotbeds of revolution. Critics snarled without let up...." Her own reception, as an unwanted and rejected child, parallels his own. And her metaphors are as acrid as Ensor's shocking colors and disagreeable content—including "Piss that streamed in a roar" "nasty and agreeable smells in placid/interiors. Lilacs and farts. Garlic and apples," "a pimple on my/rump, snot in my mouth." Ensor's defiant inclusions of the grotesque (such as decapitated heads, defecating figures, rancid smells and tastes implied in rotting flesh and food) inspires Inez's own non-idealized exploration of childhood fantasy and memory. Ensor, angry and rejected, inspires Inez to remember the confining and unaffectionate years spent in Brussels, when she was as rejected by the Sisters as the painter was by his critics. And both survived the loneliness, spinning rejection into art. In a final passage, Inez incorporates Ensor's own words in her discussion on how and why she became a poet ("to draw consoling words out of/the air.... To endure. Integral and personal"). And in another poem, "Mirror," in the same collection as her Ensor poem, Inez connects icongraphically with the painter again in her exploration of masks and skeletons that evoke the hidden depths of longing, fear, and truth lurking beneath the surface world of appearances.

Throughout her work Inez finds compelling metaphoric equivalents in art to enrich her poetry. Photographic and painterly terms and ideas layer her poetry with evocative visual and symbolic force. Ultimately, this technique pushes her autobiographical memories into a realm beyond mere personal reflection and into a broader world of human experience. Ironically, the lonely orphan finally finds kinship, lineage, family, a home.

Works Cited

Barthes, Roland. *Camera Lucida: Reflections on Photography.* Translated by Richard Howard. New York: Hill and Wang, 1983.

Hirsch, Julia. *Family Photographs: Content, Meaning, and Effect.* New York and Oxford: Oxford University Press, 1981.

Inez, Colette. "A Place at the Table," "Grandmother and Child Are Set to Listen on Sunday Nights," "The House of Dreams," "A Fairy Tale Country of Palaces," "Clemency," "The Wig of Liliane," "A Place at the Table." *Clemency: Poems by Colette Inez.* Pittsburgh, PA: Carnegie Mellon University Press, 1998.

——. "After the Cantata Sounds Its Last Alleluia," "Red August Letter," "The Dreamforest." *Family Life.* Santa Cruz, CA: Story Line Press, 1988.

——. "The Dreamforest," "Belgian Flicks," "Daughter's Photo in an Old Folks Home," "The Entry of James Ensor into My Memories of Brussels," "Mirror." *Getting Under Way: New and Selected Poems by Colette Inez.* Brownsville, OR: Story Line Press, 1993.

Lesko, Diane. *James Ensor: The Creative Years.* Princeton: Princeton University Press, 1985.

McGough, Stephen C. *James Ensor's 'The Entry of Christ into Brussels in 1889.'* New York: Garland Publishers, 1985.

Rosenblum, Robert and H.W. Janson. *19th-Century Art.* Englewood Cliffs, N.J.: Prentice-Hall, Inc., 1984.

Reviews

Rosellen Brown

Review of *Alive and Taking Names*

From *Parnassus*, Vol 1, No. 2, Spring/Summer 1973

    Colette Inez introduces her first collection with a self-advertisement wholly unnecessary if one trusts good poems to tell their own stories, to justify themselves. It embodies the best and worst of her, beginning "I write to survive the darkness by signaling my light, for music, celebration, word love, the interpretation of experience, to say people are unique as each snowflake in its palace of light melts but is never lost …" and going on through the things she and the rest of us dread: "the history of greed, glut, exploitation of the weak by those in power probably to continue and increase … Respectable men in council rooms sanctifying murder." She has, in other words, wide and not narcissistic interests, sufficient but not huge originality, a flexibility with words that can become a bit overbearing when too much is telescoped in a coyly-turned phrase, and she has genuine intensity that has found its form in many of these poems.

    The first, and very forceful, section deals with a history so symbolically charged that it would make fine fiction. But her tone, though level, conducts a quite unimaginary current of anger:

> Priest, my father, priest,
> your collar cuts my neck …
> I, your bastard child

What's so compelling here isn't the shocking confession that she was, like Hester Prynne's Pearl, "the unpremeditated outcome of a passionate moment" between a priest and a thirty-year-old virgin, who then gave her over to an orphanage, but the vividness of her telling and the unspoken depths of the degradation implied. There is fresh outrage in her—she pictures, with justifiable obsession:

> where my father stood
> in the mottled light
> of the sacristy

> fastening his cassock
> over a soul
> astounded with lust

And though she saw her mother as victim, for she

> believed her Mandrake
> his palpable cape flowing like the sky, full of cures,
>
> the miraculous church, cathedrals of illusion,
> a trunk of props and optical tricks

she still had to suffer her mother's disappearance "like a rabbit in a sleazy act." Women with plenty to bitch about at the hands of men will see the two of them, mother and daughter, as the archetypes of vulnerability: had, literally, by the man-church. Yet nonetheless a passage from "Infant Ward," which speaks, with an intensity on the order of Plath's, of "Heads of cabbage in the cribs/daily watered in a row," concludes:

> inside our throats,
> we cried to be human
> in the image of Him
> who suckled stars in Bethlehem.
> ("Cold Dust of Vestments")

A few of these poems allow an exaggeration of language that crops up sometimes as cloying sweetness ("When I was soft as ferns around the roses ... and rode my gladness high on backyard swings") and occasionally as supercharged absurdity:

> The speed below our limitations,
> we never went express, except once on the mattress
>
> unsnapping my dress, my breath's propeller turboprop
> The fullest chafing inside my wish,
> a clanging darkness, our powerhouse.
> ("Bells of St. Basil")

But the steel predominates. She is never ideological or militant, only human and hurt, whether she is writing a "Ballad to an Aborted Daughter,"

> my daughter
> blasted like a bridge
> in Scranton, Pennsylvania

or going on from that disastrous beginning full of turboprops and speed limits to show she was being wry:

> Your bones mounting mine,
> I, the plateau and you, the Tanganyikan sky bearing down,
> primate grunts and baboon refinements, the tacky room
> widening continents of heart, your hair the baboon's coat
> pressed to my face. We raided our bodies for stalks and fruit.
>
> and in my mind I tore off my skin, gave you the miles
> my intestines ran. Impasse of bones? I cracked them at the joint.
> Here, love, my tibia for your soup, my ulna for your dog,
> my heart for a stew to keep you warm.

If some of the book is less compelling—the more "public" poems could have been written by any number of poets who are outsiders to the inner city—it isn't because any themes are innately public but because Inez hasn't appropriated them fully to her deepest uses. She manages to approach her themes of urban violence and squalor with an overloaded style—busy adjectives, over-eager adverbs—that renders picturesque what she undoubtedly, with the distance of ordinary good intentions, wants us to see as deadly:

> a sidewalk's moaning migraine,
> the curb's cracked cough,
> alliterative stones singing
> charities for the dead,
> trapdoors eating beggars,
> the blistered voice of ruined men
> ("Listening with My Feet")

But when it forbears from being excessively so, much of the book is lively, the poems shaped and the language well-honed. The title poem, about a Japanese lady who refuses to tweeze her brows and disdains butterflies and senseless poems about peonies as frivolous but loves worms and slugs instead, has all Colette Inez's spirited virtues and her unfanatical appreciation of what a woman might look like in her independence—vital, sad, a little preposterous herself, being human, but essentially serious and in her own possession:

> Noon in the snow pavilion,
> gulping heated saki,
> she recalled Lord Unamuro,
> preposterous toad
> squatting by the teatray,
> proposing with conditions,
> a suitable marriage.
>
> Ha! She stoned imaginary butterflies,
> and pinching dirt,
> crawled to death's cocoon
> dragging a moth to inspect
> in the long afternoon.

Robert McDowell

Review of *Alive and Taking Names*

Hudson Review, Summer 1978

    I detect the strong air of spontaneity in the poems of Colette Inez. *Alive and Taking Names* is so rich with this quality that the poems just seem to "happen." There is considerably more at work than chance, though improvisation is the single dominant characteristic of her worst poems. But whether she is good, bad, or in-between, Inez never loses the reader's interest. Like *the* girl at the soda shop, her brazen attitude and unrestrained energy make us take notice. And like that mythical American charmer, she sometimes appears to be two entirely different individuals.

    One, the true poet, watches and comments with compassionate honesty on the world around her.

> The contained are asleep in their clouds
> but the young are like fire,
> orange and red tongues in the dark
> igniting the old from the fog of their dreams.
> ("Far in the Blindness of Time")

    The poet is involved yet not involved. She has the distance wisdom demands. She touches some chord that makes us better than we are. And her methods are so diverse! Plainly, she is in love with words. Her more formal poems contain some of the most unobtrusive—and most effective—rhymes I have seen in recent poetry. She frequently evokes the surprise image and either surpasses expectations or falls below them. She is never so predictable as to meet them. Her broad talents will lead many to conclude that she is an undisciplined writer, and there are times when the high-wire act does seem to be just for the sake of the show.

> Morf. The dog barks.
> Form for the poem.
> Meop, the cat.
> Listen to the apertures.
> Look for the throat that shapes the bark,

the mouth of the cat.

("Tunnel, Funnel, Perpendicular, Blue")

The wordplay is excessive; the total effect makes me think of Dali or a poet laureate for the Space Program. Though the writing is interesting it is not poetry. If my absolutism is offensive, perhaps we can agree it is not *good* poetry.

Good or not, when I consider the book as a whole it doesn't matter. It is good for poetry and good for Inez to push past the limits of a successful piece of writing. For when she comes back into focus, Inez comes with a deeper vision than the cozily bracketed practitioners of verse. I never get the feeling that she is writing to impress anybody; she means to test herself, to learn and make keen judgments with that knowledge in hand. When she writes poorly, when she assumes a prosaic persona and constructs topical poems that seem to be gleaned from newspapers, history books, or the experience of somebody else, I feel that the real Inez is just testing, that she will soon reclaim her own voice with an important revelation. Her curiosity is insatiable, her intuition is vibrant and somehow right. It is a joy to observe her vivid language at work. I believe that poetry, to her, is fun, and this refreshingly sets her apart from so many of the dog-faced boys. Inez is always electric, and sometimes she is at the heart of exceptional poetry.

David Lawson

A Shifting Center of Poetic Gravity

Review of *Alive and Taking Names* in *Prairie Schooner*, Volume 52, Number 3, Fall 1978

    The work of Colette Inez seems peculiarly suited to the world in which we live, since the central issues and questions of her own life are also those of perhaps more than one recent generation which has sounded a complex *leitmotif* comprising personal alienation and identity-seeking. Miss Inez's themes also fit, unmilitantly, into the general purview of feminist writings. There is some sense in which she is to poetry what Simone Weil was to theology, though such a comparison also presents difficulties. Some of the poetry of Sylvia Plath can profitably be compared with poems of Inez.

    What is a young person to do with the discovery of an intrigue which could appeal to the story writing talents of Molière, namely, that she has been discreetly placed in a Catholic orphanage by a classical-scholar mother whose lover was a Jesuit priest? One clue might be gleaned from the Sartrian notion of *project,* by which a life's trajectory may become anchored or ruddered by some specific coherence-generating activity—in this case poetry. That a confusion of cosmic proportions between biological and spiritual fatherhood could ensue appears obvious, and poetry is an appropriate means of forging clarity.

    If her first collection, *The Woman Who Loved Worms* (1972), contained psychic shards consonant with such a situation, the present volume has continuity with it, where, as in "Thinking of My Father, Priest ...":

> I've agreed to perform for the Pope
> in an aerial Vatican act. Nonsensical Nuncios.
> I'm the dunce hungry to love a priest
> on an ethereal trapeze, Daddy's stunning acrobat.

    If such a heavy mixture of absurdity and imagination accounted for all of her work, the range would be less than adequate. But her world also contains a galaxy of extra-parental figures including "Buffalo Sam," Shirley Temple, Deanna Durbin, and Hitlerian phantoms.

    Inez's familiarity with Western reaches is likely one of attunement to its mythology, via normal channels of media, which makes her "Buffalo Sam" a sardonic gloss on Western-style caricatures:

> I loved you a long time,
> Buffalo Sam,
> your oxblood chukkas
> and rifle-hard legs.

It is an overlapping mythology, that of Hollywood, and some of the comforting images once concocted there which accounts for "When Crinkled, Gold Tin Foil," with its nostalgic evocations of Shirley Temple with her "lollipops" and "dimpled white strap shoes" "tapping the sides" of a swimming pool. The same source of imagery is responsible for "Deanna Durbin, Come Home," where adolescent moviegoers of the appropriate decade inhabited balconies and "committed the dark to memory."

> As Deanna beamed, Funiculi, Funicula
> In her strapless gown
> fluttering High C:
> to our hicktown's popcorn litter.

During the same period there arose other images, ones of "the stench of the Reich," where, as in "Lieder for a Chocolate Cake":

> Every crazed taste sated, the swastika rules,
> Hitler hugging dogs, Eva taking shots
> of edelweiss in bloom, Himmler jigging
> in Wehrmacht boots as they enter the castle
> to eat swirled cakes rich as cartels.

In Inez's work there is yet another vein, a fusion of archaeology and fantasy brought alive by word-love. Readers may spot a certain cluster including "Old Woman, Eskimo," "Jungle Queen of Mato Grosso," "Mundugamor" and "The Zoroastrians Knew." The old Eskimo "has seen birth/children waiting/for their names. The Jungle Queen of Mato Grosso mixes Cleopatra with celery, carrots, and escarole into one soundscape salad. Mundugamor, who may be a verbal equivalent of "earth-love," "comes in a cape of steaming rain/Mundugamor, my father, chief." As to what the Zoroastrians knew, they knew "how men coax shadows," also what "musk for what man at dusk." The shift from "My Father, Priest" to "Mundugamor, my father, chief" could well be pivotal: the significance of this archaeological cluster, dealing as it does with primal and parental scenes, could lie in the fact that Inez is now creating a new world wherein the flesh-spirit dichotomy of an earlier poetic vein undergoes a healing fusion, yielding for her another center of gravity containing an unprecedented, vibrant source of power.

While she perhaps engages in some such new world-construction, there is still another strand worth noting in this poet's work, one centering about music, and involving such figures as Dvorak and Schoenberg. As for "Listening to Dvorak's Serenade in E":

>And this bright music
>shaping dancers
>on a bitter dust of roads,
>divining rods
>that point
>to a further distance:
>stone, water, stone.

"Schoenberg Mosaic" could be, for all we know, an attempt to set poetry to the diatonic scale. It begins with a provocative juxtaposition of "Schoenberg" and "iceberg," then develops this startling contrast of European sophistication and Arctic starkness. This poem is only one of the dozen in the fourth and final section, "Dogged Sources," where much relativity and subconscious exploration are allowed disciplined play. Quite apart from the first colorful cluster of poems which, as already noted, could be indicative of a new general direction, these last ones, invoking as they do the spirit of science and mathematics, may in themselves be taken as evidence of impending developments.

Robert DeMott

Recent Poetry

Review of *Alive and Taking Names* by Robert DeMott, *Western Humanities Review*, Volume XXXIII, Number 2, Spring 1979

If Mark Strand has built an entire cosmology on the most limited vocabulary of any major poet, Colette Inez sends one repeatedly to the dictionary. She revels in the play of language, as if the richness and abundance of diction is a positive way to fill the void of daily existence. The title poem of her second collection, *Alive and Taking Names*, celebrates the magic of words, as the final stanza shows:

> Croaker, monger, medic, quack,
> sawbones, prober, jawsmith, vet,
> I am well, sound, hale, cross referenced with fit,
> snuffling the morning air, alive and taking names.

The energy Inez taps is not the energy of self as in Sherwin, but the energy residing in language, sensation and color, which comes over to the poet in the imaginative space each poem occupies. In "November Lord" she writes,

> Time will comb the gold debris.
> Our mouths in the amber of an eon's kiss.
> But philologer, my prince sends word,
> I cross the bridge into kingdoms of light.
> Viracocha, November Lord,
> the melons are gathered beneath a gaunt moon
> which spins like my heart.

And in this rouse, "Listening to Dvorak's Serenade in E," the speaker apprehends a "further distance" of "stone, water, stone":

> Everything has ripened,
> the oranges glisten
> in their sharp worlds,

> the apples have broken
> their juice
> in my mouth,
> I am alone at the edge
> of all the gold seasons,
> a tide of clouds
> bearing me home
> like a migratory bird.

Inez's fascination with language creates pitfalls. There are several poems which are freighted by the seductive lure of words and language alone, and once again I am reminded of Stevens' observation on exoticism. They are always fun to read aloud, but their obscurity seems impenetrable. I do not understand "Selling Harvesters," "Seven Stages of Skeletal Decay," or Mya Calender …" In "Jungle Queen of Mato Grosso" we need a traffic cop to relieve the congestion:

> Those were her salad days, endive, romaine.
> Persiflage and twitting wit loudly absent
> in the hut where blanco's skull hung on a pole
> next to his bufferin, quinine and notes
> on the dreamtime of Tupis.

Inez is especially inventive with personae through which to imagine the world. "Old Woman and the War," and "Old Woman, Eskimo" are good examples. This is from the latter:

> When she stops seeing,
> the snow needles come
> sewing the land
> to the hem of the sky
> In her dream she is
> a bone needle
> that will not thread.
> The hides come undone,
> all her songs are gone
> inside the rain
> for her children
>
> to hear later on.

The most intriguing poems in the book revolve around Inez's unusual childhood. Her father was a Catholic priest, her mother an archivist. Inez came to America as a foster child just before World War II. Autobiographical elements appeared in her first book, *The Woman Who Loved Worms,* and resurface here, though with the distancing that allows her to overcome self pity and bitterness. Her execution is often uneven and oblique (so is the entire book), especially in "Pa and Ma's Rosetime Life" and "Marthe, the Mar, la Mer....", but "Twenty Song" is good and honest, and so is "Thinking of My Father, Priest, Nightflight to Home" which ends:

> So many locked away keys, how I fell
> from his highwire act into the net of these words,
> clues to his ways when he twirled off his collar
> and I was conceived, trilled stars, Paris.
>
> neon struts, le hot jazz blowing its stunts
> in the fretworks of loss
> where my father made the sign.

Robert Schultz

"Full Throated Assurance"

Review of *Getting Under Way: New and Selected Poems* in *The Hudson Review*, Volume XLVII Number 3, Autumn 1994

In *Getting Under Way: New and Selected Poems* by Colette Inez, there is a book within the book. Inez's poetry is cosmopolitan in its interests and various in its modes, but it returns repeatedly to a central story which is at once personal and archetypal. It is the story of Inez's own parentage, childhood, and growth into maturity, and it is the story of the making and sustaining of a coherent self in spite of destructive circumstances.

Inez is the daughter of an archival scholar and a Catholic priest. At birth, she was placed in a Brussels orphanage where she remained for eight years. Just before the outbreak of World War II, she was sent to a foster family in the United States. In this country, her first foster mother died of alcoholism and her second was abusive. The sheer narrative is compellingly presented in poems scattered throughout the career. The earliest of these tend to be complaints or protests, as in "A Collar Round My Thoughts," which begins: "Priest, my father, priest,/your collar cuts my neck...." Ten years later, in her third book, she is able to write poems which confront the parents she did not know, seeking to wring from them, if only in her own imagination, a necessary acknowledgment. In "Along the Garonne," she writes:

> In my mother's room ghosts sighed:
>
> "Who are you to make claims?"
> "Lovechild," I answer in a river town
> of cypress and palm,
> floodmarks on the house
> from an old spring torrent.

The breakthrough volume in this narrative is *Family Life* (1988), in which Inez turns her gaze most directly upon her childhood, her parents, and her foster parents. And it is in this volume that she achieves an impressive poise, fashioned out of understanding, pity, and forgiveness for her biological and foster parents, all of whom she has surpassed in maturity and self-possession.

A turning point is revealed in the poem "The Dream Forest," in which the young girl decides to become "rich in words." She is newly arrived in the United States and does not understand the English spoken around her by disapproving foster grandparents, so she resorts to her imagination and commits herself to a mastery of her new language. And so it is by means of poetry that she is, in *Family Life,* able to imagine and forgive her unknown parents. Reflecting upon her poetic vocation in a more recent poem ("The Entry of James Ensor into My Memories of Brussels"), she writes:

> ... the child I was asks: what am I to learn in the subtle
> world? And I answer her, to draw consoling words out of
> the air. To arrange them like irises in a vase, to weave
> them into proof our lives like a sea teem
> with remembrances. To endure....

The 37 new poems included in the selected poems indeed teem with remembrances, as Inez continues to recover her past and to reconcile herself more fully to it. Some of the poems continue strands of significant imagery. One, "Santa Cruz Idyll," imagines her parents together, with herself watching, "stirring my image at the edge of a pond." Later in the same poem: "Now I stand near the water that touched their bodies when they swam." From the "spring torrent" that marked her mother's imagined house, to the river that touches her parents' bodies as they swim in her vision of them, water has signified the illicit passion of her conception. It is also the reflective element in which she has tried, with difficulty, to perceive herself. In the mirror-less orphanage she tried at dinner to glimpse herself in the liquid in her bowl, and she and a friend "squatted by a puddle and wrote our names/on water with a stick ..." Though the names vanished, "The reflected sky trembled with our signatures" ("Escape from the Iron Gates"). In many poems throughout the career, mirrors and water recur in an ongoing meditation upon names, writing, and identity.

One of the achievements of Inez's career is that it traces the progress of a poet from choked protest to full-throated assurance. Over time, the poet has presented herself as one whose "resonating breath" was cut off by her priest-father's collar, then as a girl writing her name in water, and finally as "a visible woman, full of inventions." This is a triumphant progress beautifully rendered, and the present collection, in which we can trace it, is very welcome. But I think there is room for yet another book. This second selected poems would deliberately gather and arrange only the autobiographical poems, including some not found in the present volume, into the poetic *Bildungsroman* which stands at the center of this splendid career.

Scott Edward Anderson

"The Agony and Enlightenment of a Complete Life"

Review of *Getting Under Way: New and Selected Poems* in *The Bloomsbury Review*, Volume 14/Issue 6, Nov./Dec. 1994

The early work of the generation of poets whose first collections appeared in the seventies can be an extremely frustrating read. This is not to say that there are no collections from the "me-decade" that still pass muster—certainly Robert Hass' *Field Guide* (Yale Series of Younger Poets, 1973), Stephen Dobyns' *Concurring Beasts* (Atheneum, 1972), and Charles Wright's second volume, *Hard Freight* (Wesleyan University, 1973), stand the test of contemporary scrutiny. Many other poets, however, were lost at sea in the wake of the openly confessional experiments of Lowell and Berryman and the freeform self-absorption of the Beats.

The seventies were a transitional time for American poetry, indeed for American culture, and the urbane surrealism that marks so much of that poetry now seems ingenuous, if not downright self-conscious. It is dated work, some of which our discerning and arguably more sophisticated palates can't stomach.

How, then, are we to approach the work of another poet of that generation who has loosed the trappings of her time, whose work has gained in experience and facility? *Getting Under Way: New and Selected Poems* by Colette Inez poses just such a challenge.

We can take some satisfaction in this poet's struggle, which has taken her over some choppy waves, from the claustrophobia of

> Service for two,
> I shall dine with myself.
> Duchess of pity
> demitasse cups;
> mother-of-pearl on the knives
> that I may cut
> my mother in half
> like a Florida prawn.
> ("Service for Two, I Shall Dine with Myself")

to the more open waters of

> She won't look
> into my eyes. I'll watch her turn away
> after I leave. A flutter of a memory
> too swift to catch will vanish in a meadow,
> a corridor of trees. Was it her face
> bent over my crib? Were her shoulders
> hunched when she whispered to the priest?
> What did she confess to him?
> ("Gascon Journey")

What distinguishes Colette Inez is her frenetic perception and crash-and-burn technique. It is a manner that opens her up to potential failure, but often yields a startling clarity,

> In slow Motion, my body turns
> through a keyhole of light
> out of the forest and into the meadow.
> Springtails and mites
> seem to study slantwise light on moss
> like geometers.
> In a margin of grass, a cricket stops
> to revise its ancient argument.
> ("Skokie River Cadenzas")

Inez's work is about survival and personal growth through the agony and enlightenment of a complex life. She deftly handles many personal demons—from a childhood of abuse in foster homes to reckoning with her unconventional parentage (she was born to a scholar and a Catholic priest). Through it all, her work is informed by a playfulness that is emblematic of her hard-won existence.

Her compass is set for true north, whether aimed at her own life or at the wasteland of our society. She utilizes razor-sharp powers of description, which are often trained on the natural world, as in "Lines for Eastern Bluebirds":

> bluebirds seizing beetles, crickets
> in loose snarls of grass,

roosting in orchards,
on high tension lines over back roads,
piping variations
in sloughed over double notes
where loosestrife flares against a sky
wanting no particular reply
to katydids' debate: do they burn
the same blue, the summer day,
did they, do they, learn blue, bluebird, jay?

While many lesser poets were swept away in the littoral undertow of the seventies, Hass, Dobyns, and Wright all survived to write some of their finest work. Colette Inez, judging by the poems in *Family Life* (Story Line Press, 1988) and the recent work represented in *Getting Under Way*, has claimed a seat next to them in the lifeboat.

Steven Styers

"The Reconstruction of a Life"

Review of *Clemency* in *West Branch*, 43

Mild weather, that's what clemency can mean, or mercy. But to get to that one usually has to go through some kind of storm. Colette Inez's *Clemency* is the reconstruction of a life. Her years of searching for clues to her identity is the mortal storm that results in discovering her father was a priest and meeting the mother who gave her up for adoption. Her clemency is for that past, those inscrutable parents, and also, finally, for herself. Such material could hold melodrama, but in Inez's *Clemency* there is a deeply felt and communicated mercy. She has a different story to tell, a true one, however implausible, but a true story nevertheless, reshaped through the art of her poetry. Beneath the calm surface of her poems is the turmoil out of which her autobiography was born, the piecing together of a denied family history, and all that energy that would become the poet. In "Refrain for My Sires" she reconceives her conception and birth:

> Water. Mary Mother blue. Ashes of rose.
> Fish doze in deep pools, baptismal silver.
> I, born from these lovers' bodies,
>
> would swim out of their spasms and cries.
> I can never tell them, embraced in their gaze,
> I too have wept in dry grass
>
> beneath stars like rue anemones in the open woods,
> I, who was born from these lovers' bodies,
> closed eyes, tongue numb, their flesh in the grass.

The words remind us of the sheer physicality of life's beginnings, that all flesh is grass, momentarily in existence, holding moments of passion, having consequences.

She may have never really understood the father she never knew and the mother who didn't want her, the mother who later could never quite accept her as a daughter, but she comes to an acceptance of who they were and a kind of forgiveness. There is also a sweet revenge in the quiet satisfaction of revealing to the world what her parents wanted to keep so secret. She does this without bitterness but with genuine emotion. In "Word Circuits, Solitary" she recalls the tenacity of her need to know where she came from:

> It was her habit to correct my letters,
> crossing out errors in red ink. My French
> on the page bled from its wounds but stumbled on
> like a courier carrying a message that refused to be lost. Lost and
> Found....

And later in the poem she considers what all those words meant, what they will mean:

> ... Everything they said
> about birth is dead or waits to be reborn.
>
> Why do I muse on the question: is death a shift
> of chemicals? Look for my atoms in a school of fish,
> a distant snow, a nebula's veil in a diffuse dream
>
> in the marriage of great galaxies. Language, a stay
> against death....

In "The Perseid Meteors of August" she places all of our personal dramas, all we care about so much, the past and the future, in the proper context of a universe that does not care:

> One then another, they hurtle over the barn
> beyond farm lights and outlying reaches of town.
> Tipped into earth they jostle the dreams
> of our ancestors
>
> and the about-to-be-born who are crowning.
> Blood smeared, out of their mothers' pods
> they hammer the air with cries
> to the heaven overhead that does not see them.

In the face of ultimate futility and isolation, Inez tells us we are people struggling to know who we are, who must care about each other, and who must carry on in an implausible, indifferent, but splendid cosmos.

For Further Reading

Charlotte Alexander. "Current Books of Poetry." Review of *The Woman Who Loved Worms*. *Poet Lore*, spring, 1973.

Dennis Bernstein. "The Poetry Worm: A Portrait of Colette Inez." *Helicon Nine*, 1984.

Richard Caram. Review of *The Woman Who Loved Worms*. *Open Places*, winter, 1973.

Thomas Carren. Review of *Clemency*. *Prairie Schooner*, summer, 2001.

Kelly Cherry. "Sidestepping Wreckage." Review of *Alive and Taking Names*. *Parnassus*, fall/winter, 1978.

Mary Anna Dunn. Review of *The Woman Who Loved Worms*. *Voyages*, volume 5, 1973.

Kenny Fries. Review of *Clemency*. *Harvard Review*, fall, 2000.

Mary Carter Ginn. "Colette Inez Has Her Say in *Clemency*." *Miller's Pond*, volume 3, 2000.

Jim Gorman. Review of *Alive and Taking Names*. *Three Rivers Poetry Journal*, March, 1978.

Karla M. Hammond. "An Interview with Colette Inez." *Nimrod*, volume 24, number 1, fall/winter, 1980.

Marcia Lee Masters. Review of *The Woman Who Loved Worms*. Chicago Tribune, May 10, 1972.

Palmer Hasty. Review of *Eight Minutes from the Sun*. *Prairie Schooner*, fall 1985.

Beverlee Hughes and Virginia Elson. "Conversation with Colette Inez." *Yes: A Magazine of Poetry*, spring, 1973.

Sydney Lea. Review of *Eight Minutes from the Sun*. *Paintbrush*, volumes 11&12, numbers

21&24, 1984 & 1985.

—. "Maturities." Review of *Clemency*. *The Georgia Review,* fall 1998.

Mary Elsie Robertson and Stan Sanvel Rubin. "'The Sheer Extravagance of Pineapple': A Conversation with Colette Inez." *Kalliope*, volume 12, number 2, 1990.

Richard Simpson. "Visible Women, Full of Inventions." Review of *Getting Under Way*. *Tar River Poetry*, fall, 1994.

J.D. Smith. Review of *Clemency*. *Chelsea*, 67, spring, 2000.

Pamela Stewart. Review of *Alive and Taking Names*. *Raccoon*, 7, May, 1980.

Robert Joe Stout. "Real People, Real Feelings." Review of *Alive and Taking Names*. *Southwest Review*, volume 64, number 2, spring, 1979.

Henry Taylor. Review of *Alive and Taking Names*. *The Hollins Critic*, volume 15, number 2, April, 1978.

Barbara Unger. "The Craft of Writers." Review of *Eight Minutes from the Sun*. *Contact II*, winter, 1986.